STEPHEN had the face and heart of a boy, the temper of a martyr, the zeal of fire; he was the first Christian martyr, the forerunner of Paul.

PAUL grasped the ends of the ancient world and bound them to the Cross.

PHILIP preached to great crowds, and to a lonely government servant.

SILAS preached with Paul, faced mobs by day and prison by night.

TIMOTHY: Paul used him as courier for his messages and trusted him with the ruling of the church at Ephesus.

These men and others, beloved by God, martyred for the sake of Christ, were the first builders of the Christian Church.

Here is the sixth in the unique series that brings all of the excitement, drama and color of the Bible in words and pictures from the world's greatest, truest Book!

D1307472

The Picture Bible for All Ages

VOLUME 6

THE CHURCH

ACTS — REVELATION

Script by Iva Hoth

Illustrations by Andre Le Blanc

Bible Editor, C. Elvan Olmstead, Ph.D.

David C. Cook Publishing Co.
850 NORTH GROVE AVENUE • ELGIN, IL 60120
In Canada: David C. Cook Publishing (Canada) Ltd., Weston, Ontario M9L 1T4

THE CHURCH
First printing, June 1973
© 1973 David C. Cook Publishing Co., Elgin, IL 60120
All Rights Reserved. This book, or parts thereof,
may not be reproduced in any form without permission
of the publisher, except by a reviewer who wishes
to quote brief passages in connection with a review
in a magazine or newspaper.
Published by David C. Cook Publishing Co.
Printed in United States of America by Offset Paperbacks.
Library of Congress Catalog Card Number: 73-78173
ISBN: 0-912692-18-9

ILLUSTRATED STORIES

THE CHURCH

*And the Lord
added to the church daily
such as should be saved.*

ACTS 2: 47

The Acts of the Apostles,

THE FIFTH BOOK OF THE NEW TESTAMENT, TELLS HOW JESUS' DISCIPLES OBEYED HIS COMMAND TO GO INTO ALL THE WORLD AND PREACH THE GOSPEL.

Waiting for a Promise FROM ACTS 1: 1-26

FORTY DAYS AFTER HIS RESURRECTION JESUS TAKES HIS ELEVEN DISCIPLES TO THE MOUNT OF OLIVES, NEAR BETHANY. WHILE HE IS GIVING THEM HIS FINAL BLESSING, HE IS LIFTED UP OUT OF THEIR SIGHT. IN AWE AND WONDER THEY STAND LOOKING UP INTO HEAVEN AS IF TO CATCH ONE MORE GLIMPSE OF THE MASTER THEY LOVE. SUDDENLY TWO ANGELS APPEAR.

YOU MEN OF GALILEE, WHY DO YOU STAND HERE LOOKING UP INTO HEAVEN-- JESUS WILL COME AGAIN-- IN THE VERY WAY YOU HAVE SEEN HIM GO.

THE ANGELS DISAPPEAR, AND PETER TURNS TO THE OTHERS.

LET'S DO WHAT JESUS TOLD US TO DO-- GO BACK TO JERUSALEM AND WAIT FOR THE POWER HE PROMISED TO SEND US BEFORE WE BEGIN HIS WORK.

SO THE DISCIPLES, WHO HAD ONCE FLED FOR FEAR OF BEING ARRESTED AS FRIENDS OF JESUS, RETURN TO THE CITY-- KNOWING THAT JESUS IS DEPENDING ON THEM TO CARRY ON THE WORK FOR WHICH HE WAS CRUCIFIED.

IN JERUSALEM THEY TAKE LODGING IN AN UPPER ROOM WHICH SOON BECOMES A MEETING PLACE FOR OTHER FOLLOWERS OF JESUS.

JUDAS, WHO BETRAYED OUR LORD, IS DEAD. WE SHOULD APPOINT SOMEONE TO TAKE HIS PLACE.

I NOMINATE BARSABAS.

MATTHIAS.

THE DISCIPLES ASK GOD'S GUIDANCE IN THE CHOICE THEY MAKE -- AND MATTHIAS IS NAMED.

THE LORD HAS BLESSED YOU, MATTHIAS.

FOR THE NEXT TEN DAYS THE DISCIPLES MEET TOGETHER IN PRAYER--WAITING FOR THE COMING OF THE HOLY SPIRIT. AT THE SAME TIME FAITHFUL JEWS FROM ALL OVER PALESTINE, AND EVEN DISTANT COUNTRIES, CROWD INTO JERUSALEM TO CELEBRATE THE FEAST OF THANKSGIVING CALLED PENTECOST.

MANY OF THE PILGRIMS PASS BY THE PLACE CALLED CALVARY, AND ARE REMINDED OF JESUS' CRUCIFIXION.

ROMAN SOLDIERS SAY JESUS' DISCIPLES STOLE HIS BODY FROM THE TOMB AND CLAIM HE ROSE FROM THE DEAD AS HE PROPHESIED HE WOULD.

BUT I'VE ALSO HEARD THAT A LOT OF PEOPLE SAW JESUS--ALIVE. I HOPE I CAN FIND SOMEONE IN JERUSALEM WHO DID.

I'M SEEKING THE TRUTH--BUT IT WILL TAKE A SIGN FROM GOD TO MAKE ME BELIEVE THAT JESUS' DISCIPLES SPEAK IT.

11

Like Tongues of Fire

FROM ACTS 2: 1-38

THESE QUESTIONS ARE STILL BEING ASKED AS JEWS COME TO JERUSALEM TO CELEBRATE THE HARVEST FEAST CALLED PENTECOST. JESUS' DISCIPLES KNOW THE TRUTH; BUT THEY ARE WAITING FOR POWER FROM GOD TO HELP THEM PREACH IT TO THE WORLD

WAS JESUS RAISED FROM THE DEAD? OR DID HIS DISCIPLES STEAL HIS BODY FROM THE TOMB AND CLAIM THAT HE WAS?

EARLY ON THE DAY OF PENTECOST 120 FOLLOWERS OF JESUS ARE GATHERED IN A SECRET ROOM, PRAYING. SUDDENLY THERE IS A SOUND LIKE A RUSHING, MIGHTY WIND, AND GOD'S PRESENCE FILLS THE ROOM. THEN, LIKE TONGUES OF FIRE, HIS SPIRIT RESTS ON EACH ONE.

13

14

Three Thousand in a Day

FROM ACTS 2: 38—3: 7

WHEN PETER BOLDLY TELLS THE PEOPLE IN JERUSALEM THAT THEY CONDEMNED GOD'S CHOSEN ONE TO DIE, THEY ASK, "WHAT CAN WE DO?" "REPENT AND BE BAPTIZED IN THE NAME OF THE ONE YOU CRUCIFIED," PETER REPLIES. ONE BY ONE THE PEOPLE CRY OUT...

O GOD, FORGIVE MY SINS, IN THE NAME OF YOUR SON, JESUS CHRIST, WHO CAME TO SAVE ME!

YOU SAID ONLY A SIGN FROM GOD COULD MAKE YOU BELIEVE JESUS' DISCIPLES SPOKE THE TRUTH--

YES, AND I HAVE SEEN THAT SIGN. I BELIEVE JESUS LIVES. I BELIEVE HE IS THE SON OF GOD AND THAT THROUGH HIM MY SINS CAN BE FORGIVEN. HOW GOOD GOD IS TO GIVE ME A CHANCE TO BEGIN A NEW LIFE -- WITH JESUS!

16

ONE AFTERNOON WHEN PETER AND JOHN GO TO THE TEMPLE FOR PRAYER THEY FIND A LAME MAN BEGGING AT THE BEAUTIFUL GATE.

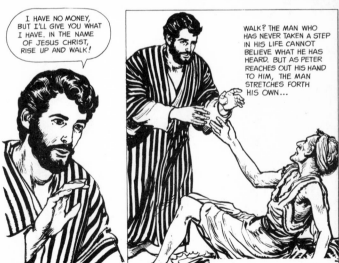

WALK? THE MAN WHO HAS NEVER TAKEN A STEP IN HIS LIFE CANNOT BELIEVE WHAT HE HAS HEARD. BUT AS PETER REACHES OUT HIS HAND TO HIM, THE MAN STRETCHES FORTH HIS OWN...

17

Miracle at the Gate

FROM ACTS 3: 7—4: 17

TO THE LAME BEGGAR AT THE TEMPLE GATE, PETER HOLDS OUT HIS HAND AND SAYS, "IN THE NAME OF JESUS CHRIST, RISE UP AND WALK!" AT ONCE THE MAN FEELS STRENGTH COME INTO HIS LEGS AND ANKLES. HE LEAPS TO HIS FEET!

I CAN WALK! PRAISE GOD, I CAN WALK!

18

In his excitement THE MAN RUSHES INTO THE TEMPLE, LEAPING AND SHOUTING FOR JOY.

LOOK! ISN'T THAT THE LAME MAN WHO WAS AT THE GATE?

YES, BUT--

GRATEFULLY, THE MAN TURNS TO PETER AND JOHN. THE CROWDS GATHER AROUND-- EAGER TO KNOW WHAT HAS HAPPENED.

WHY DO YOU LOOK AT US AS THOUGH **WE** MADE THIS MAN WALK? THE HEALING POWER CAME FROM GOD, WHO HAS DONE THIS TO HONOR JESUS WHOM **YOU** CRUCIFIED, BUT GOD RAISED FROM THE DEAD.

Seeing THAT HE HAS THE ATTENTION OF THE CROWD, PETER CONTINUES...

REPENT, AND TURN TO GOD SO THAT YOUR SINS MAY BE WIPED OUT. PREPARE YOURSELVES, FOR CHRIST WILL COME AGAIN...

AT THE BACK OF THE CROWD THE PRIESTS LISTEN. THEY ARE ANGRY—AND THEIR ANGER INCREASES AS THEY WATCH THE GROWING INTEREST OF THE PEOPLE.

HE MUST BE STOPPED AT ONCE--OR HE'LL HAVE ALL OF JERUSALEM BELIEVING THAT JESUS ROSE FROM THE DEAD.

WITH THE HELP OF THE CAPTAIN OF THE TEMPLE GUARDS, THE PRIESTS PUSH THEIR WAY THROUGH THE CROWDS.

YOU ARE UNDER ARREST!

WITHOUT ANOTHER WORD, PETER AND JOHN ARE MARCHED AWAY TO PRISON-- BUT ALREADY FIVE THOUSAND MEN HAVE DECLARED THEIR BELIEF IN JESUS.

THE NEXT MORNING THEY ARE BROUGHT BEFORE THE SANHEDRIN, THE SAME JEWISH COURT THAT CON-DEMNED JESUS TO DEATH. BESIDE THEM-- PERFECTLY WELL-- STANDS THE MAN WHO HAD BEEN LAME FROM BIRTH.

BY WHAT POWER AND IN WHOSE NAME HAVE YOU HEALED THIS MAN?

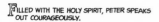

FILLED WITH THE HOLY SPIRIT, PETER SPEAKS OUT COURAGEOUSLY.

LET IT BE KNOWN TO YOU, AND ALL THE PEOPLE OF ISRAEL-- THIS MAN WAS HEALED BY THE NAME OF JESUS CHRIST OF NAZARETH, WHOM **YOU** CRUCIFIED!

THE COURT IS STUNNED. PETER AND JOHN ARE UNEDUCATED FISHERMEN, YET THEY SPEAK AND ACT WITH AUTHORITY AND POWER.

TAKE THEM AWAY --UNTIL WE CALL FOR THEM AGAIN.

THE MINUTE THE PRISONERS ARE OUT OF SIGHT, THE COURT HOLDS A MEETING.

EVERYONE KNOWS A MIRACLE HAS TAKEN PLACE. WE CANNOT DENY IT, BUT WE MUST KEEP THE NEWS FROM SPREADING. WHAT CAN WE DO?

TELL THESE "PREACHERS" THAT IF THEY SPEAK AGAIN IN THE NAME OF JESUS THEY WILL BE PUT TO DEATH AS HE WAS!

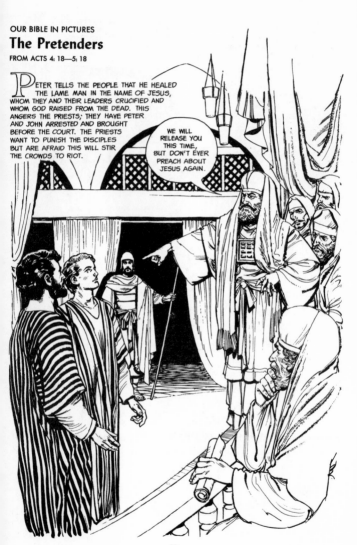

OUR BIBLE IN PICTURES

The Pretenders

FROM ACTS 4: 18—5: 18

PETER TELLS THE PEOPLE THAT HE HEALED THE LAME MAN IN THE NAME OF JESUS, WHOM THEY AND THEIR LEADERS CRUCIFIED AND WHOM GOD RAISED FROM THE DEAD. THIS ANGERS THE PRIESTS; THEY HAVE PETER AND JOHN ARRESTED AND BROUGHT BEFORE THE COURT. THE PRIESTS WANT TO PUNISH THE DISCIPLES BUT ARE AFRAID THIS WILL STIR THE CROWDS TO RIOT.

WE WILL RELEASE YOU THIS TIME, BUT DON'T EVER PREACH ABOUT JESUS AGAIN.

WHETHER IT IS RIGHT IN THE EYES OF GOD FOR US TO OBEY HIM OR YOU, YOU MUST DECIDE. BUT WE HAVE TO KEEP ON PREACHING WHAT WE HAVE SEEN AND HEARD.

SUCH BOLDNESS ANGERS THE PRIESTS EVEN MORE, BUT AFTER THREATENING THE DISCIPLES AGAIN, THEY LET THEM GO. PETER AND JOHN HURRY BACK TO THEIR FRIENDS WHO IMMEDIATELY JOIN THEM IN PRAYER.

O GOD, GIVE US COURAGE TO SPEAK THY WORD FEARLESSLY.

STRENGTHENED BY THE POWER OF THE HOLY SPIRIT, THE DISCIPLES KEEP ON PREACHING. MORE AND MORE PEOPLE JOIN THEIR FELLOWSHIP. ONE DAY A MAN NAMED BARNABAS BRINGS THE DISCIPLES A LARGE BAG OF MONEY.

WHY ARE YOU GIVING ALL THIS MONEY TO US?

I SOLD MY LAND, AND I WANT THE MONEY USED TO HELP THE FOLLOWERS OF JESUS WHO ARE IN NEED.

THE PRAISE THAT IS SHOWERED ON BARNABAS FOR HIS GENEROUS GIFT PROMPTS A MAN NAMED ANANIAS AND HIS WIFE, SAPPHIRA, TO SEEK SUCH HONOR FOR THEMSELVES.

WE, TOO, HAVE SOLD OUR LAND AND WE WANT TO GIVE THE MONEY TO HELP THE CHURCH.

ANANIAS, THE MONEY WAS YOURS TO DO WITH AS YOU PLEASED. BUT WHY DO YOU PRETEND TO GIVE ALL, WHEN YOU KNOW THAT IS NOT TRUE? DON'T YOU SEE -- YOU ARE LYING TO GOD?

WHEN ANANIAS HEARS THESE WORDS, HE FALLS DOWN DEAD. SOME YOUNG MEN TAKE HIS BODY AWAY, AND AS THEY ARE RETURNING SAPPHIRA COMES IN. LIKE HER HUSBAND, SHE LIES ABOUT THE MONEY.

SAPPHIRA, YOUR HUSBAND IS DEAD BECAUSE HE LIED TO GOD. AND YOU WILL PAY THE SAME PENALTY.

INSTANTLY SAPPHIRA FALLS TO THE FLOOR -- AND DIES. THE FOLLOWERS OF JESUS LOOK ON THIS SEVERE PUNISHMENT AS A WARNING TO ANYONE WHO THINKS HE CAN PRETEND LOYALTY TO GOD.

IN SPITE OF THREATS, THE DISCIPLES KEEP ON HEALING IN THE NAME OF JESUS. THE PRIESTS WATCH--ANGRY BUT HELPLESS--AS FAMILIES BRING THEIR SICK ONES OUT INTO THE STREETS, WAITING FOR THE DISCIPLES TO PASS BY AND HEAL THEM.

HE IS LAME— PLEASE MAKE HIM STRONG SO THAT HE CAN RUN AND PLAY LIKE OTHER CHILDREN.

I CANNOT HEAL HIM, BUT JESUS, THE SON OF GOD, CAN. IN HIS NAME, I SAY TO YOU, YOUR SON IS HEALED.

THE FAME OF THE DISCIPLES SPREADS-- AND SOON PEOPLE FROM THE TOWNS ROUND ABOUT CROWD INTO JERUSALEM, BEGGING TO BE HEALED. AT LAST THE PRIESTS CAN STAND IT NO LONGER. IN A FIT OF RAGE THEY HAVE THE DISCIPLES ARRESTED AND THROWN INTO JAIL.

THIS TIME THERE WILL BE NO RELEASE!

Missing Prisoners

FROM ACTS 5: 19—6: 10

AFRAID THAT THE CROWDS MIGHT TURN AGAINST THEM, THE PRIESTS ARE FORCED TO STAND BY WHILE JESUS' DISCIPLES CONTINUE TO TEACH AND HEAL THE SICK. BUT WHEN PEOPLE FROM OTHER CITIES BEGIN TO POUR INTO JERUSALEM ASKING FOR THE DISCIPLES, THE PRIESTS CAN CONTROL THEIR JEALOUSY NO LONGER. THEY HAVE THE DISCIPLES ARRESTED AND THROWN INTO PRISON. DURING THE NIGHT AN ANGEL FROM GOD RELEASES THEM.

GO-- STAND IN THE TEMPLE AND TELL PEOPLE ABOUT THE NEW LIFE GOD HAS PROMISED THOSE WHO BELIEVE IN HIS SON, JESUS CHRIST.

THE NEXT MORNING THE HIGH PRIEST CALLS THE JEWISH COURT INTO SESSION AND ORDERS THE DISCIPLES BROUGHT BEFORE IT. WHEN THE OFFICERS RETURN...

THE PRISON IS LOCKED AND THE GUARDS ARE ON DUTY! BUT WHEN WE OPENED THE DOORS THERE WAS NO ONE THERE!

NOT THERE? WHERE ARE THEY?

AT THAT MOMENT A PRIEST ENTERS THE ROOM.

THE MEN YOU PUT IN JAIL LAST NIGHT ARE IN THE TEMPLE TEACHING ABOUT JESUS!

THE HIGH PRIEST ORDERS THE DISCIPLES BROUGHT TO THE COURT AT ONCE.

DIDN'T WE WARN YOU NOT TO PREACH ABOUT JESUS?

27

WE MUST OBEY GOD RATHER THAN MEN!

AT THIS REPLY THE COURT IS SO ANGRY THAT IT WANTS THE DISCIPLES KILLED AT ONCE. BUT GAMALIEL, A FAMOUS TEACHER, QUICKLY ORDERS THE DISCIPLES TAKEN OUTSIDE. THEN HE TURNS TO THE COURT.

BE CAREFUL OF THE ACTION YOU TAKE AGAINST THESE MEN. IF THIS TEACHING IS THEIR OWN IDEA, IT WILL FAIL. BUT IF IT IS FROM GOD YOU CANNOT DEFEAT THEM -- AND YOU WILL FIND YOURSELVES IN THE AWFUL POSITION OF FIGHTING GOD.

THE COURT IS FORCED TO ADMIT THE WISDOM OF THIS ADVICE. ANGRILY IT ORDERS THE DISCIPLES BEATEN, THEN RELEASES THEM WITH A THREAT OF MORE PUNISHMENT IF THEY CONTINUE PREACHING ABOUT JESUS.

THE DISCIPLES LEAVE...

I'M PROUD TO BE ABLE TO SUFFER FOR JESUS. WE'LL KEEP RIGHT ON WORKING FOR HIM.

ONE OF THEM -- STEPHEN -- IS SOON RECOGNIZED AS A FINE PREACHER.

IN SPITE OF THREATS THE DISCIPLES GO ON PREACHING AND HEALING. THE NUMBER OF FOLLOWERS INCREASES SO MUCH THAT THE TWELVE DISCIPLES DECIDE OTHERS MUST BE CHOSEN TO HELP WITH THE WORK. SEVEN DEACONS ARE SELECTED.

HIS FORMER FRIENDS IN THE SYNAGOGUE CHALLENGE HIM TO A DEBATE ABOUT JESUS. TO THEIR EMBARRASSMENT THEY FIND THEY ARE NO MATCH FOR STEPHEN'S WISDOM AND ABILITY TO DEFEND HIS FAITH. SECRETLY THEY PLOT THEIR REVENGE.

WE MUST BE CAREFUL NOT TO TURN THE PEOPLE AGAINST US.

RIGHT -- BUT IF WE HANDLE IT PROPERLY WE CAN USE THE PEOPLE THEMSELVES TO HELP US DESTROY STEPHEN.

29

Martyr for Christ

FROM ACTS 6: 11—8: 4

STEPHEN PREACHES SUCH POWERFUL SERMONS THAT MANY PEOPLE IN JERUSALEM BECOME FOLLOWERS OF JESUS.

THE JEWISH TEACHERS CHALLENGE HIM TO DEBATES, BUT THEY ARE NO MATCH FOR HIM. THIS MAKES THEM ANGRY, AND THEY PLOT TO GET RID OF HIM.

HERE'S SOME MONEY—SPREAD THE WORD AROUND JERUSALEM THAT STEPHEN IS PREACHING AGAINST THE LAW GOD GAVE TO MOSES.

THAT WILL TURN EVERY GOOD JEW IN JERUSALEM AGAINST STEPHEN.

THE PLOT WORKS -- STEPHEN IS ARRESTED AND BROUGHT BEFORE THE SANHEDRIN, THE SAME COURT THAT CONDEMNED JESUS TO DEATH.

BOLDLY STEPHEN ANSWERS HIS ENEMIES...

YOUR FATHERS PERSECUTED THE PROPHETS WHO TOLD ABOUT THE COMING OF GOD'S CHOSEN ONE-- AND NOW **YOU** HAVE MURDERED **HIM**. **YOU** ARE THE ONES WHO RECEIVED GOD'S LAW, AND **YOU** ARE THE ONES WHO HAVE DISOBEYED IT!

REMEMBERING THE APOSTLES' STRANGE ESCAPE FROM PRISON, THE PERSECUTORS SEEM AFRAID TO ARREST THEM. BUT RAIDS AGAINST THE OTHER DISCIPLES CONTINUE, AND THEY ARE FORCED TO FLEE FOR THEIR LIVES.

WE MUST ESCAPE AT ONCE. I'M NOT A COWARD, BUT MY FAMILY--

JESUS SAID THAT IF WE WERE PERSECUTED IN ONE CITY WE SHOULD FLEE TO ANOTHER.

TWO BIG CARAVANS ARE LEAVING BY THE NORTH GATE TOMORROW MORNING. IF WE'RE CAREFUL WE CAN JOIN THEM AND NOT BE SEEN.

EARLY THE NEXT MORNING TRADERS LEAD THEIR CAMEL TRAINS OUT OF THE CITY, AND IN THEIR MIDST...

WHEREVER WE GO WE'LL TAKE OUR FAITH IN JESUS WITH US.

AND AS WE TEACH OTHERS WE'LL BE HELPING TO SPREAD THE GOSPEL AS JESUS ASKED US TO DO.

AND SO, BY DRIVING JESUS' FRIENDS OUT OF JERUSALEM, JEWISH LEADERS, UNKNOWINGLY, CAUSE HIS TEACHINGS TO BE SPREAD THROUGHOUT ALL PALESTINE--EVEN AMONG THEIR ENEMIES, THE SAMARITANS!

Simon, the Magician

FROM ACTS 8: 5-26

To escape persecution at the hands of the Jewish leaders, thousands of Jesus' followers flee from Jerusalem. Philip, one of the deacons of the Jerusalem church, goes north to Samaria.

SAMARITANS HATE JEWS. BUT THEY, TOO, ARE LOOKING FOR A SAVIOR, SO I MUST TELL THEM THAT HE HAS COME.

To Philip's surprise the Samaritans listen eagerly as he tells them about Jesus, and they watch with wonder as he lovingly heals their sick.

IN THE NAME OF JESUS CHRIST, STAND UP AND WALK!

I CAN STAND--ALONE! TELL ME MORE ABOUT JESUS SO THAT I CAN BECOME HIS FOLLOWER, TOO.

SOON, EVERYONE IN SAMARIA IS TALKING ABOUT PHILIP.

SIMON, THIS MAN PHILIP CAN DO GREATER THINGS THAN YOU CAN. HE CAN HEAL THE SICK, MAKE THE LAME WALK, AND--

HE CAN? WHERE CAN I FIND HIM?

SIMON, THE MOST FAMOUS MAGICIAN IN SAMARIA, HURRIES OFF TO FIND PHILIP.

I THOUGHT I KNEW ALL THE TRICKS OF MAGIC.

WHEN HE FINDS PHILIP HE WATCHES WITH AMAZEMENT THE MIRACLES OF HEALING. BUT HE ALSO LISTENS TO WHAT PHILIP SAYS, AND AFTER A WHILE...

I BELIEVE IN JESUS, TOO. BAPTIZE ME, AND LET ME GO WITH YOU TO LEARN MORE.

WHEN REPORTS OF PHILIP'S WORK REACH THE DISCIPLES IN JERUSALEM, PETER AND JOHN GO TO VISIT SAMARIA. AND AS THEY LAY THEIR HANDS ON THESE NEW FRIENDS OF JESUS, THE HOLY SPIRIT COMES UPON THEM.

THIS IS THE MOST WONDERFUL THING I HAVE EVER SEEN.

SELL ME THIS POWER THAT YOU HAVE.

SIMON! MONEY WILL NOT BUY THIS HOLY GIFT. YOU HAVE NO PLACE IN GOD'S WORK, FOR I CAN SEE THAT YOUR HEART IS FILLED WITH WICKEDNESS. REPENT, AND PRAY THAT GOD WILL FORGIVE YOU.

THE BIBLE DOES NOT SAY WHETHER SIMON TRULY REPENTS. HIS NAME IS NEVER MENTIONED AGAIN.

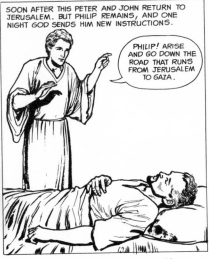

SOON AFTER THIS PETER AND JOHN RETURN TO JERUSALEM. BUT PHILIP REMAINS, AND ONE NIGHT GOD SENDS HIM NEW INSTRUCTIONS.

PHILIP! ARISE AND GO DOWN THE ROAD THAT RUNS FROM JERUSALEM TO GAZA.

WITHOUT KNOWING THE REASON FOR HIS JOURNEY, OR WHERE IT MAY TAKE HIM, PHILIP OBEYS...

On the Gaza Road

FROM ACTS 8: 26-40; 9: 31-35

"GO DOWN TO THE ROAD THAT LEADS TO GAZA," AN ANGEL OF GOD TELLS PHILIP. PHILIP OBEYS, AND AS HE WALKS ALONG THE HOT DESERT HIGHWAY A CHARIOT COMES UP BEHIND HIM. HE LOOKS BACK, AND AT THAT MOMENT THE HOLY SPIRIT SPEAKS TO HIM: "GO UP TO THE CHARIOT--AND KEEP CLOSE TO IT."

WHO COULD BE IN THAT CHARIOT THAT GOD HAS SENT ME ALL THIS WAY TO MEET?

AGAIN PHILIP OBEYS. NEARING THE CHARIOT, HE HEARS A MAN READING FROM THE SCRIPTURES.

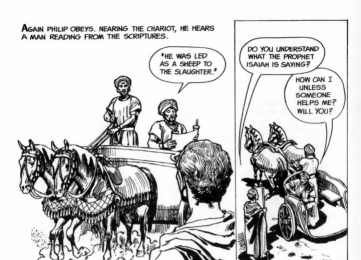

"HE WAS LED AS A SHEEP TO THE SLAUGHTER."

DO YOU UNDERSTAND WHAT THE PROPHET ISAIAH IS SAYING?

HOW CAN I UNLESS SOMEONE HELPS ME? WILL YOU?

EAGERLY PHILIP GETS INTO THE CHARIOT. THE MAN INTRODUCES HIMSELF AS TREASURER FOR CANDACE, QUEEN OF ETHIOPIA. THEN HE TURNS BACK TO THE SCROLL.

IS THE PROPHET TALKING ABOUT HIMSELF-- OR SOMEONE ELSE?

ABOUT JESUS CHRIST, THE SON OF GOD. HIS ENEMIES CRUCIFIED HIM, BUT GOD RAISED HIM FROM THE DEAD.

As they ride along Philip explains that God loved the world so much that he sent his son Jesus to die for our sins, and whoever trusts in him will live forever with God.

I believe in Jesus, and I'm sorry for everything wrong I have done. Is there any reason why I cannot be baptized and become one of his followers?

I'm sure that's what God sent me here to do.

So the man from Ethiopia is baptized... and then he continues his journey, eager to tell the good news about Jesus to his own people.

Philip goes north, preaching in the towns along the rim of the Mediterranean Sea. In Caesarea, the Roman capital in Palestine, he makes his home.

About this time a miraculous thing happens--Paul, who has been persecuting Jesus' friends, has a wonderful experience. On the way to Damascus, Jesus appears to him. Paul knows that Jesus is the savior whom God raised from the dead. So, instead of persecuting Jesus' followers, Paul becomes a follower, too.

When the disciples hear this they rejoice, for now they can travel all over Palestine teaching and healing in the name of Jesus without fear of Paul arresting them.

Sea of Galilee

CAESAREA

JOPPA
LYDDA
JERUSALEM

GAZA

MEDITERRANEAN SEA

Dead Sea

WHILE PETER IS PREACHING IN LYDDA...

MY FRIEND, AENEAS, HAS BEEN PARALYZED FOR EIGHT YEARS. CAN YOU HELP HIM?

I CAN'T-- BUT THE SON OF GOD CAN. COME, LET'S GO SEE YOUR FRIEND.

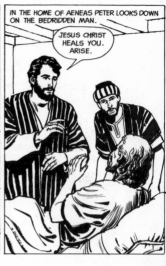

IN THE HOME OF AENEAS PETER LOOKS DOWN ON THE BEDRIDDEN MAN.

JESUS CHRIST HEALS YOU. ARISE.

AENEAS STANDS UP. HE LOOKS IN AWE AT HIS STRONG ARMS AND LEGS.

JESUS MUST LOVE ME VERY MUCH TO RESTORE MY STRENGTH. TELL ME MORE ABOUT HIM SO THAT I CAN BECOME HIS FOLLOWER, TOO.

WHEN THE PEOPLE SEE AENEAS--WELL AND STRONG --THEY BELIEVE IN JESUS, TOO. PETER STAYS IN LYDDA, PREACHING, UNTIL ONE DAY TWO MEN FROM THE SEAPORT OF JOPPA ARRIVE IN THE CITY.

WHERE'S PETER? WE MUST FIND HIM AT ONCE!

Mission to Joppa

FROM ACTS 9: 36—10: 2

WHILE PETER IS PREACHING IN LYDDA TWO MEN FROM JOPPA COME TO HIM WITH AN URGENT REQUEST:

"DORCAS, ONE OF JESUS' FOLLOWERS, JUST DIED. YOU RESTORED AENEAS' HEALTH; CAN YOU HELP DORCAS?" PETER GOES WITH THE MEN AT ONCE, AND WHEN THEY REACH JOPPA...

HER BODY HAS BEEN PLACED IN THE ROOM UPSTAIRS.

41

AT THE SIGHT OF DORCAS SOME OF THE WOMEN FALL ON THEIR KNEES, WEEPING FOR JOY. OTHERS RUSH OUT INTO THE STREETS TO TELL THE EXCITING NEWS.

DORCAS IS ALIVE!

SHH-- PEOPLE WILL THINK YOU'RE LOSING YOUR MIND. DORCAS IS DEAD-- AND EVERYONE KNOWS IT.

NO! NO! PETER, THE DISCIPLE OF JESUS, BROUGHT HER BACK TO LIFE. COME, SEE FOR YOURSELF!

NOT BELIEVING, BUT CURIOUS, THE WOMAN HURRIES TO DORCAS' HOME.

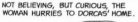

IT'S TRUE! IT'S TRUE! OH, GOD BE PRAISED!

THE NEWS SPREADS QUICKLY THROUGHOUT JOPPA, AND SOON GREAT CROWDS COME TO PETER, BEGGING TO BE TAUGHT ABOUT JESUS. PETER CONTINUES TO PREACH IN JOPPA UNTIL...

ONE DAY A STRANGE THING HAPPENS IN THE HOME OF CORNELIUS, A ROMAN CENTURION LIVING IN THE SEACOAST CITY OF CAESAREA, SOME THIRTY MILES NORTH. IT IS THREE O'CLOCK IN THE AFTERNOON. CORNELIUS, WHO IN HIS YEARS OF SERVICE IN PALESTINE HAS LEARNED TO WORSHIP GOD, KNEELS TO PRAY.

God, a Roman, and a Jew

FROM ACTS 10: 2—11: 1

43

HE, TOO, HAS A VISION. AND A VOICE COMMANDS HIM: "GET UP, PETER; KILL AND EAT."

NEVER, LORD. IN ALL MY LIFE I HAVE NEVER EATEN ANYTHING THAT THE JEWISH LAW CALLS UNCLEAN.

THE VOICE REPLIES: "YOU MUST NOT CALL WHAT GOD HAS CLEANSED UNCLEAN." ALL THIS IS REPEATED THREE TIMES; THEN THE VISION DISAPPEARS. WHILE PETER IS WONDERING WHAT IT MEANS THE HOLY SPIRIT SPEAKS TO HIM: "THREE MEN ARE HERE LOOKING FOR YOU. GO WITH THEM AND HAVE NO DOUBTS, FOR I HAVE SENT THEM TO YOU."

PETER HURRIES DOWNSTAIRS-- AND FINDS THREE MEN AT THE GATE INQUIRING FOR HIM.

I AM THE MAN YOU ARE LOOKING FOR. WHAT DO YOU WANT?

CORNELIUS, A ROMAN CENTURION WHO WORSHIPS GOD, WAS COMMANDED BY AN ANGEL TO SEND FOR YOU.

THE NEXT DAY PETER AND SIX OF HIS FRIENDS SET OUT WITH THE THREE MEN FOR CAESAREA. AS THEY ENTER THE HOME OF CORNELIUS, THE ROMAN CENTURION FALLS ON HIS KNEES TO WORSHIP PETER.

NO--NO-- I AM A MAN LIKE YOURSELF.

THEY ENTER THE HOUSE--AND FIND IT FILLED WITH ROMANS.

ACCORDING TO JEWISH LAW, GENTILES--YOU PEOPLE OF ANOTHER NATION--ARE UNCLEAN. THEREFORE, AS A JEW, I AM FORBIDDEN TO ASSOCIATE WITH YOU. BUT GOD HAS TOLD ME IN A VISION THAT NO MAN MUST BE CALLED UNCLEAN. SO I HAVE COME AS YOU ASKED. WHAT DO YOU WANT OF ME?

AN ANGEL OF GOD TOLD ME TO SEND FOR YOU. AND WE ARE WAITING TO LEARN WHAT THE LORD HAS COMMANDED YOU TO TELL US.

I SEE NOW THAT ANY MAN, JEW OR GENTILE, WHO LOVES GOD AND DOES WHAT IS RIGHT, IS ACCEPTABLE TO HIM.

SUCH NEWS TRAVELS FAST, AND WHEN IT REACHES THE CHURCH IN JERUSALEM...

HOW DARE PETER BREAK JEWISH LAWS AND ASSOCIATE WITH GENTILES?

THEN PETER TELLS THEM THAT JESUS WAS THE SAVIOR SENT FROM GOD TO GIVE ETERNAL LIFE TO ALL WHO BELIEVE IN HIM. WHEN PETER SEES THAT THE HOLY SPIRIT HAS COME TO THE GENTILES, HE HAS HIS CHRISTIAN FRIENDS BAPTIZE THEM.

Angel–Open Gate

FROM ACTS 11: 1—12: 14

THE NEWS THAT PETER HAS BEEN ASSOCIATING WITH GENTILES REACHES JERUSALEM BEFORE HE DOES--AND SEVERAL OF THE CHURCH MEMBERS ARE WAITING TO QUESTION HIM.

IS IT TRUE THAT YOU ARE BREAKING OUR JEWISH LAWS AND BEING FRIENDLY TOWARD GENTILES--EVEN EATING WITH THEM AND VISITING IN THEIR HOMES?

GOD DIRECTED A ROMAN CENTURION TO SEND FOR ME, AND GOD TOLD ME TO GO TO HIM. I OBEYED, AND WHILE I WAS TELLING THE GENTILES ABOUT JESUS, THE HOLY SPIRIT CAME TO THEM -- THE SAME AS TO US ON THE DAY OF PENTECOST. IF GOD GAVE THEM THE SAME GIFT THAT HE GAVE TO US, WHO WAS I TO STAND IN THE WAY?

THE MEMBERS AGREE WITH PETER -- AND PRAISE GOD FOR GIVING ETERNAL LIFE TO THE GENTILES. THE CHURCH CONTINUES TO GROW...

AND AS IT DOES THE ANGER OF THE JEWISH LEADERS GROWS. TO WIN THEIR FAVOR, KING HEROD AGRIPPA BEGINS TO PERSECUTE JESUS' FOLLOWERS.

ARREST THE DISCIPLE CALLED JAMES. CHARGE HIM WITH STIRRING UP TROUBLE AND PUT HIM TO DEATH-- AT ONCE!

SO JAMES, ONE OF THE FOUR FISHERMEN WHO LEFT THEIR NETS TO FOLLOW JESUS, IS SLAIN TO SATISFY A WICKED KING'S STRUGGLE FOR POWER.

THIS PLEASES THE JEWISH LEADERS WHO CONDEMNED JESUS TO DEATH. EAGER TO GAIN MORE OF THEIR FAVOR, HEROD ORDERS PETER ARRESTED AND PUT IN PRISON --TO BE EXECUTED AFTER THE FEAST OF THE PASSOVER.

CHAIN EACH HAND TO A GUARD. KEEP FOUR SOLDIERS ON WATCH AT ALL TIMES. THIS PRISONER **MUST NOT** ESCAPE!

BUT ON THE NIGHT BEFORE HEROD PLANS TO SENTENCE PETER, AN ANGEL OF GOD ENTERS THE PRISON CELL...

GET UP! PUT ON YOUR SANDALS, WRAP YOUR CLOAK AROUND YOU, AND FOLLOW ME.

AS PETER OBEYS THE CHAINS FALL FROM HIS WRISTS -- AND THE ANGEL LEADS HIM OUT OF THE PRISON CELL.

WHEN THEY APPROACH THE GREAT IRON GATE IN THE PRISON WALL, IT OPENS! THEY GO OUT INTO THE CITY STREETS, AND -- SUDDENLY -- THE ANGEL VANISHES!

SCARCELY BELIEVING WHAT HAS HAPPENED, PETER HURRIES TO THE HOME OF MARY, THE MOTHER OF HIS YOUNG FRIEND, MARK. THERE HE POUNDS ON THE DOOR OF THE GATE UNTIL RHODA, A SERVANT GIRL, ANSWERS.

IT'S PETER!

BUT INSTEAD OF LETTING HIM IN, RHODA TURNS AND RUNS BACK INTO THE HOUSE...

OUR BIBLE IN PICTURES
Fall of a Tyrant
FROM ACTS 12: 14-24

IT IS NIGHT IN JERUSALEM. PETER HAS JUST BEEN RESCUED FROM PRISON BY AN ANGEL AND IS SEEKING ADMITTANCE AT THE HOME OF A FRIEND. WHEN THE SERVANT GIRL RECOGNIZES HIS VOICE, SHE RUSHES BACK INTO THE HOUSE.

IT'S PETER!

PETER? O RHODA, YOU'RE SO UPSET THAT YOU'RE IMAGINING THINGS.

THE GIRL INSISTS. FINALLY SOME OF THE GROUP, WHO HAVE GATHERED TO PRAY FOR PETER, ACCOMPANY HER TO THE GATE.

IF YOU KNEW IT WAS PETER, WHY DIDN'T YOU LET HIM IN?

I WAS SO EXCITED-- I HAD TO TELL YOU.

CAUTIOUSLY THEY OPEN THE DOOR...

PETER! IT **IS** YOU! COME IN--QUICKLY!

DID HEROD RELEASE YOU?

NO-- BUT GOD DID. AN ANGEL AWAKENED ME AND TOLD ME TO FOLLOW. I DID-- AND THE PRISON GATES OPENED BEFORE US. IN THE STREET, THE ANGEL DISAPPEARED. TELL THE OTHERS THAT I AM FREE. AND NOW I MUST GET OUT OF JERUSALEM BEFORE HEROD LEARNS WHAT HAS HAPPENED.

THE FRIENDS OF PETER REJOICE AND THANK GOD FOR HIS ESCAPE, BUT THE NEXT MORNING WHEN HEROD DISCOVERS THAT HIS PRISONER IS GONE--

YOU SAY HE WAS CHAINED TO TWO GUARDS, AND OTHERS WERE GUARDING THE DOOR, YET YOU EXPECT ME TO BELIEVE THAT HE JUST DISAPPEARED? WHAT WERE THE GUARDS DOING? SEARCH THE CITY. FIND PETER OR THOSE TRAITORS WILL PAY FOR THIS WITH THEIR LIVES!

BUT THE SEARCH FAILS.

50

A FEW DAYS LATER HEROD APPEARS AT A PUBLIC CELEBRATION IN CAESAREA. THERE, DRESSED IN A DAZZLING ROBE OF SILVER, HE GOES OUT AND SPEAKS TO THE PEOPLE. TO FLATTER HIM, THEY SHOUT:

IT IS THE VOICE OF A GOD--NOT A MAN!

HEROD ACCEPTS THE PRAISE WHICH SHOULD HAVE BEEN GIVEN ONLY TO GOD. SUDDENLY GOD STRIKES HIM DOWN, AND A FEW DAYS LATER HE DIES.

WITH THE DEATH OF HEROD, THE PERSECUTION OF THE CHURCH STOPS FOR A TIME. THE GOOD NEWS OF JESUS CHRIST CONTINUES TO SPREAD THROUGHOUT THE LAND OF THE JEWS...

The Story of Paul

Adventurer for Christ

BOLDLY HE FACES ANGRY MOBS... CROSSES MOUNTAINS... AND SAILS
THE STORMY SEAS TO PREACH THE GOOD NEWS THAT JESUS
IS THE SON OF GOD AND SAVIOR OF THE WORLD.

THE EXCITING STORY OF
THIS GREAT MISSIONARY
BEGINS LONG AGO...

A FEW YEARS AFTER THE BIRTH OF JESUS PAUL* IS BORN IN TARSUS. THE SON OF GOOD JEWISH PARENTS, HE IS BROUGHT UP TO WORSHIP AND OBEY GOD.

WHAT WILL YOU DO WHEN YOU GROW UP, PAUL?

I DON'T KNOW YET. BUT WHATEVER I DO, IT WILL BE FOR GOD, AND IT WILL BE EXCITING.

*HIS JEWISH NAME IS SAUL.

HE TAKES THE FIRST STEP TOWARD MAKING HIS DREAM COME TRUE WHEN HE GOES TO JERUSALEM TO STUDY. THERE HE MEETS SOME OF THE SAME TEACHERS THAT JESUS TALKED WITH ONLY A FEW YEARS BEFORE.

IN TIME PAUL BECOMES THE MOST BRILLIANT PUPIL OF THE FAMOUS TEACHER, GAMALIEL. TOGETHER THEY DISCUSS THE SCRIPTURES-- ESPECIALLY THE PARTS THAT TELL ABOUT THE COMING OF THE SAVIOR.

LIKE KING DAVID, HE WILL MAKE OUR COUNTRY STRONG AND POWERFUL. IF ONLY HE WOULD COME NOW -- I'D SPEND MY LIFE SERVING HIM.

BUT LIKE MOST JEWISH LEADERS, PAUL REFUSES TO ACCEPT JESUS AS THE SAVIOR FOR WHOM THE JEWS ARE WAITING. WHEN THEY STONE STEPHEN, ONE OF JESUS' FOLLOWERS, PAUL STANDS BY -- WATCHING.

ANY MAN WHO FOLLOWS JESUS DESERVES TO DIE!

PAUL SOON BEGINS HIS OWN ATTACK ON JESUS' FOLLOWERS. HE RAIDS THEIR HOMES AND DRAGS THEM OFF TO BE QUESTIONED, PUNISHED, EVEN PUT TO DEATH.

NO! NO! MY CHILDREN!

THE FOLLOWERS OF JESUS FLEE FOR THEIR LIVES. WHEN PAUL LEARNS THAT THEY ARE SPREADING THEIR TEACHING WHEREVER THEY GO, HE IS EVEN MORE FURIOUS.

THEY MUST BE STOPPED BEFORE THEY STIR UP PEOPLE EVERYWHERE. ALREADY THEY ARE AS FAR NORTH AS DAMASCUS.

WHAT CAN WE DO?

With some strong-armed men, Paul sets out on a 190-mile journey to Damascus. His excitement mounts with every mile, for he believes with all his heart that in destroying Jesus' followers he is serving God...

A Light and a Voice

PAUL RIDES TOWARD DAMASCUS WITH THE EAGERNESS OF A HUNTER ON THE TRACK OF HIS PREY. AT THE SIGHT OF THE CITY IN THE DISTANCE, HE URGES HIS HORSE ON -- AS IF EVERY MINUTE COUNTED IN HIS SEARCH TO DESTROY JESUS' FOLLOWERS.

SUDDENLY HE IS SURROUNDED BY A LIGHT BRIGHTER THAN THE NOONDAY SUN. HE FALLS TO THE GROUND -- AND A VOICE CALLS HIM BY HIS JEWISH NAME: "SAUL! SAUL, WHY ARE YOU PERSECUTING ME?"

WHO ARE YOU?

I AM JESUS OF NAZARETH, WHOM YOU ARE PERSECUTING.

WHAT DO YOU WANT ME TO DO?

"GO INTO THE CITY," JESUS ANSWERS, "AND YOU WILL BE TOLD WHAT TO DO."

57

58

59

Damascus Plot

FROM ACTS 9: 23-26

BEHIND CLOSED DOORS IN THE CITY OF DAMASCUS, AN UGLY PLOT IS BORN.

PAUL CAME TO DAMASCUS TO HELP US GET RID OF THE FOLLOWERS OF JESUS. INSTEAD HE HAS BECOME ONE OF THEM. HE'S A TRAITOR...

BUT A BRILLIANT ONE-- WHICH MAKES HIM EVEN MORE DANGEROUS. WE HAVE TO GET RID OF HIM BEFORE HE CONVINCES MORE PEOPLE THAT THIS JESUS WHO WAS CRUCIFIED IS THE SON OF GOD.

CAREFULLY THE MURDER PLANS ARE MADE-- BUT THE SECRET LEAKS OUT.

PAUL! I'VE JUST LEARNED THAT THERE IS A PLOT TO KILL YOU!

I SUSPECTED THIS. I'LL LEAVE AT ONCE.

NO! NO! OUR ENEMIES HAVE SECURED THE HELP OF THE GOVERNOR HIMSELF. EVERY GATE OF THE CITY IS GUARDED. BUT I HAVE A PLAN—STAY IN HIDING UNTIL I CAN WORK IT OUT.

CAUTIOUSLY, THROUGHOUT THE DAY, THE WORD IS SPREAD TO SOME OF JESUS' FOLLOWERS.

TONIGHT—AT THE FIRST HOUSE BY THE SOUTH WALL.

THAT NIGHT PAUL'S FRIENDS GATHER AT THE HOUSE BY THE WALL.

THEY PRAY TOGETHER, AND THEN...

61

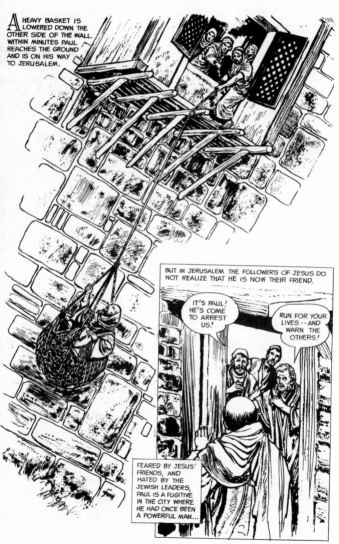

A HEAVY BASKET IS LOWERED DOWN THE OTHER SIDE OF THE WALL. WITHIN MINUTES PAUL REACHES THE GROUND AND IS ON HIS WAY TO JERUSALEM.

BUT IN JERUSALEM THE FOLLOWERS OF JESUS DO NOT REALIZE THAT HE IS NOW THEIR FRIEND.

IT'S PAUL! HE'S COME TO ARREST US!

RUN FOR YOUR LIVES -- AND WARN THE OTHERS!

FEARED BY JESUS' FRIENDS, AND HATED BY THE JEWISH LEADERS, PAUL IS A FUGITIVE IN THE CITY WHERE HE HAD ONCE BEEN A POWERFUL MAN...

OUR BIBLE IN PICTURES
Man with a Mission
FROM ACTS 9: 27-30; 11: 22-25

PAUL RETURNS TO JERUSALEM ONLY TO FIND THAT JESUS' FRIENDS BELIEVE HE IS STILL THEIR ENEMY. AT THE SIGHT OF HIM THEY HIDE. BUT BARNABAS, THE MAN WHO SOLD HIS FARM AND GAVE THE MONEY FOR THE POOR, IS NOT AFRAID. HE LISTENS TO PAUL -- AND TAKES HIM TO PETER.

PAUL SAYS HE IS NOW A FOLLOWER OF JESUS -- AND I BELIEVE HIM.

BRING HIM IN.

FOR DAYS AND NIGHTS PAUL, THE BRILLIANT STUDENT OF JEWISH LAW, AND PETER, THE RUGGED FISHERMAN FROM GALILEE, TALK ABOUT THEIR LORD AND SAVIOR.

JESUS' LAST COMMAND DIRECTED US TO GO INTO ALL THE WORLD AND PREACH THE GOSPEL.

I'M GLAD HE TRUSTS ME TO HELP CARRY OUT THAT COMMAND.

64

BUT JESUS' FOLLOWERS AGAIN LEARN OF THE PLOT AGAINST PAUL'S LIFE, AND WARN HIM.

YOUR ENEMIES ARE POWERFUL MEN, PAUL, AND THEY WILL NOT STOP UNTIL THEY HAVE PUT AN END TO YOUR WORK IN JERUSALEM. LET US HELP YOU ESCAPE.

YOU ARE RIGHT! I CAN SERVE MY LORD ELSEWHERE.

WITH THE HELP OF FRIENDS, PAUL ESCAPES TO THE SEACOAST. THEN HE SAILS NORTH TO HIS BOYHOOD HOME OF TARSUS. THERE HE EARNS HIS LIVING BY MAKING TENTS -- AND DEVOTES THE REST OF HIS TIME TO TELLING PEOPLE THAT JESUS IS THE PROMISED SAVIOR.

ONE DAY A SHIP DOCKS AT TARSUS... A PASSENGER HURRIES DOWN THE PLANK.

NOW TO FIND PAUL!

65

IN ANTIOCH, THE THIRD LARGEST CITY OF THE ROMAN EMPIRE, PAUL AND BARNABAS WIN BOTH JEWS AND GENTILES TO FAITH IN CHRIST. HERE THE FOLLOWERS OF JESUS ARE GIVEN THE NAME OF CHRISTIANS!

AFTER A TIME TEACHERS FROM JERUSALEM COME TO VISIT THE GROWING CHURCH. ONE OF THEM, AGABUS, MAKES A TRAGIC PROPHECY.

I HAVE RECEIVED A WARNING FROM GOD THAT A GREAT FAMINE IS COMING. MANY OF OUR PEOPLE IN JERUSALEM ARE POOR. THEY WILL STARVE UNLESS--

PAUL INTERRUPTS EXCITEDLY.

LET US ALL GIVE WHAT MONEY WE CAN. I'LL HELP DELIVER IT!

BUT YOU HAVE ENEMIES IN JERUSALEM!

AND OUR LORD HAS FOLLOWERS THERE! WE MUST HELP THEM IN SPITE OF THE DANGER.

68

69

The Enemy Strikes

FROM ACTS 13: 7-50

AFTER A TOUR ACROSS THE ISLAND OF CYPRUS, PAUL, BARNABAS, AND YOUNG MARK REACH THE CAPITAL. TO THEIR SURPRISE, THE ROMAN GOVERNOR CALLS THEM BEFORE HIM AND ASKS TO HEAR ABOUT JESUS. EAGERLY PAUL TELLS ABOUT JESUS AND HOW GOD RAISED HIM FROM THE DEAD. AT THIS THE COURT MAGICIAN RISES UP IN ANGER...

LIES! ALL LIES! NO MAN CAN DIE AND LIVE AGAIN!

YOU CHILD OF THE DEVIL! IT IS TIME YOU STOPPED TRYING TO TURN PEOPLE FROM THE RIGHT WAYS OF THE LORD. NOW HIS HAND IS UPON YOU-- AND FOR A TIME YOU WILL BE BLIND!

71

72

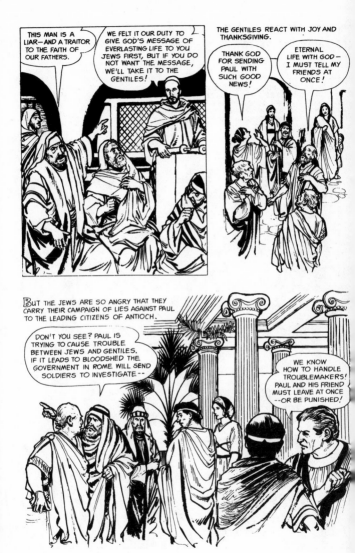

73

Miracle in Lystra

FROM ACTS 13: 51—14: 19

TO ESCAPE PERSECUTION, PAUL AND BARNABAS ARE FORCED TO LEAVE ANTIOCH. THEY GO SOUTHEAST ABOUT 80 MILES TO ICONIUM, ANOTHER CITY IN THE PROVINCE OF GALATIA. THERE JEWS AND GREEKS ALIKE ACCEPT THE GOOD NEWS OF JESUS. THIS ANGERS THE JEWISH LEADERS --

PAUL! BARNABAS! YOU MUST LEAVE AT ONCE! THERE'S A PLOT UNDER WAY TO STONE YOU!

DON'T WORRY -- YOU HAVE FRIENDS HERE WHO WILL FIGHT TO PROTECT YOU.

WE CANNOT LET YOU RISK YOUR LIVES FOR US. WE MUST LEAVE -- BUT KEEP STRONG IN YOUR FAITH, AND HELP THE OTHERS.

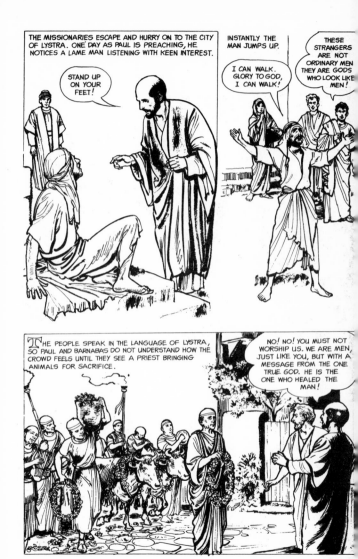

75

BUT YOU ARE LIKE THE GODS JUPITER AND MERCURY.

JUPITER AND MERCURY ARE FALSE GODS. WORSHIP THE TRUE GOD WHO HAS SENT YOU RAIN FROM HEAVEN AND FRUIT IN ITS SEASON.

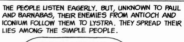

THE PEOPLE LISTEN EAGERLY. BUT, UNKNOWN TO PAUL AND BARNABAS, THEIR ENEMIES FROM ANTIOCH AND ICONIUM FOLLOW THEM TO LYSTRA. THEY SPREAD THEIR LIES AMONG THE SIMPLE PEOPLE.

PAUL AND BARNABAS CAUSE TROUBLE WHEREVER THEY GO. GET RID OF THEM AS WE DID!

THERE'LL BE NO TROUBLE IN LYSTRA. I'LL SEE TO THAT!

SO A MOB IS WHIPPED INTO ACTION!

THERE'S PAUL! STONE HIM!

Storm Warning

FROM ACTS 14: 19—15: 1

WHIPPED INTO A RAGE BY MEN FROM ANTIOCH AND ICONIUM, THE PEOPLE OF LYSTRA TURN AGAINST PAUL AND STONE HIM.

77

WHEN THE STONING IS FINISHED, THE ANGRY MOB DRAGS PAUL'S BODY OUT OF THE CITY.

QUICKLY BARNABAS AND CHRISTIANS OF LYSTRA GATHER AROUND PAUL'S MOTIONLESS FORM. BUT AS THEY STAND WEEPING...

HE'S GETTING UP! THANK GOD, HE LIVES! HE LIVES!

PAUL! WE THOUGHT THEY HAD KILLED YOU!

THEY MEANT TO, BUT GOD HAS SAVED MY LIFE FOR A PURPOSE. COME, LET'S GO BACK INTO THE CITY.

BACK TO LYSTRA? THAT MOB WILL NEVER LET YOU OUT ALIVE!

GOD WILL PROTECT ME.

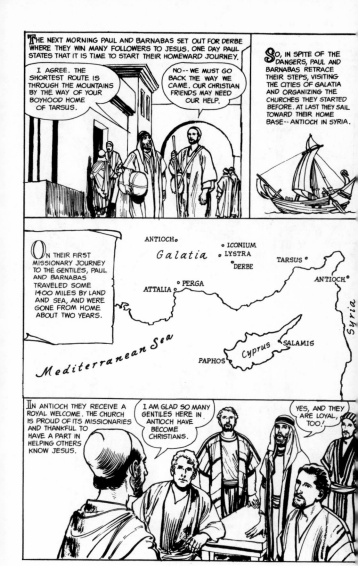

WITH PAUL AND BARNABAS AS LEADERS, THE CHURCH IN ANTIOCH GROWS IN SIZE AND INFLUENCE. BUT ONE DAY A GROUP OF JEWISH CHRISTIANS FROM THE CHURCH IN JERUSALEM ARRIVES.

YOU GENTILES CANNOT BECOME CHRISTIANS UNLESS YOU FIRST PROMISE TO OBEY OUR JEWISH LAWS!

BY WHAT AUTHORITY DO YOU SAY THAT?

BY THE AUTHORITY OF JAMES, THE BROTHER OF JESUS, WHO IS NOW LEAD IN THE CHURCH IN JERUSALEM.

HOW CAN THIS BE TRUE? PAUL DOES NOT SAY SO. WHAT SHALL WE DO?

I DON'T KNOW. I'LL NEVER GIVE UP MY FAITH IN JESUS, BUT I CAN'T OBEY ALL THOSE JEWISH LAWS.

THEN YOU CANNOT BE A CHRISTIAN!

THE QUARREL GROWS -- JEWISH CHRISTIANS VERSUS GENTILE CHRISTIANS. THE CHURCH IN ANTIOCH IS IN DANGER OF SPLITTING IN TWO!

Council in Jerusalem

FROM ACTS 15: 1-13; GALATIANS

LIKE A VIOLENT WIND, A DISAGREEMENT BETWEEN THE JEWISH AND GENTILE CHRISTIANS RIPS THROUGH THE ANTIOCH CHURCH, DIVIDING THE MEMBERS. UNKNOWN TO PAUL AND BARNABAS, WHO ARE STRUGGLING TO KEEP THE CHURCH UNITED, ANOTHER STORM IS BUILDING UP IN THE AREA OF THEIR FIRST MISSIONARY JOURNEY...

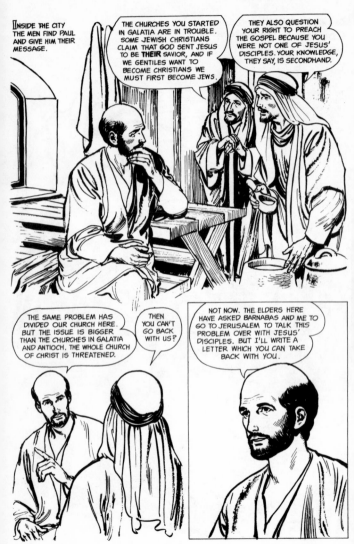

INSIDE THE CITY THE MEN FIND PAUL AND GIVE HIM THEIR MESSAGE.

THE CHURCHES YOU STARTED IN GALATIA ARE IN TROUBLE. SOME JEWISH CHRISTIANS CLAIM THAT GOD SENT JESUS TO BE **THEIR** SAVIOR, AND IF WE GENTILES WANT TO BECOME CHRISTIANS WE MUST FIRST BECOME JEWS.

THEY ALSO QUESTION YOUR RIGHT TO PREACH THE GOSPEL BECAUSE YOU WERE NOT ONE OF JESUS' DISCIPLES. YOUR KNOWLEDGE, THEY SAY, IS SECONDHAND.

THE SAME PROBLEM HAS DIVIDED OUR CHURCH HERE. BUT THE ISSUE IS BIGGER THAN THE CHURCHES IN GALATIA AND ANTIOCH. THE WHOLE CHURCH OF CHRIST IS THREATENED.

THEN YOU CAN'T GO BACK WITH US?

NOT NOW. THE ELDERS HERE HAVE ASKED BARNABAS AND ME TO GO TO JERUSALEM TO TALK THIS PROBLEM OVER WITH JESUS' DISCIPLES. BUT I'LL WRITE A LETTER WHICH YOU CAN TAKE BACK WITH YOU.

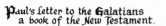

*Paul, an apostle... unto the churches of Galatia:
Why are you turning away from the good news of Jesus
which you so gladly accepted? What I preached to you was not
an idea of men. It was revealed to me by Christ. God called me
to be an apostle to preach to other nations. You don't have to
keep the Jewish laws in order to be a Christian. Those who
are trying to take away your freedom and make you live as
Jews are only causing trouble. My trust is in Christ, who
died on the cross to set us free from evil.*

THE DECLARATION OF SPIRITUAL
INDEPENDENCE PUT FORTH IN THIS
LETTER MADE CHRISTIANITY A RELIGION FOR
ALL PEOPLE RATHER THAN JUST FOR THE JEWS.

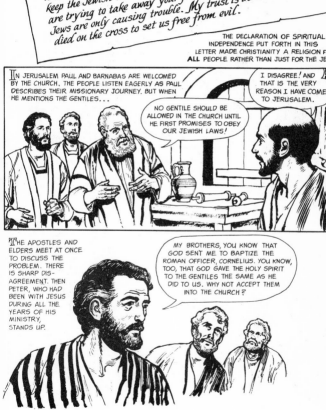

IN JERUSALEM PAUL AND BARNABAS ARE WELCOMED BY THE CHURCH. THE PEOPLE LISTEN EAGERLY AS PAUL DESCRIBES THEIR MISSIONARY JOURNEY. BUT WHEN HE MENTIONS THE GENTILES...

I DISAGREE! AND THAT IS THE VERY REASON I HAVE COME TO JERUSALEM.

NO GENTILE SHOULD BE ALLOWED IN THE CHURCH UNTIL HE FIRST PROMISES TO OBEY OUR JEWISH LAWS!

THE APOSTLES AND ELDERS MEET AT ONCE TO DISCUSS THE PROBLEM. THERE IS SHARP DISAGREEMENT. THEN PETER, WHO HAD BEEN WITH JESUS DURING ALL THE YEARS OF HIS MINISTRY, STANDS UP.

MY BROTHERS, YOU KNOW THAT GOD SENT ME TO BAPTIZE THE ROMAN OFFICER, CORNELIUS. YOU KNOW, TOO, THAT GOD GAVE THE HOLY SPIRIT TO THE GENTILES THE SAME AS HE DID TO US. WHY NOT ACCEPT THEM INTO THE CHURCH ?

PAUL CONTINUES THE REPORT OF HIS MISSIONARY JOURNEY.

IN OUR MISSIONARY TRAVELS THE HOLY SPIRIT LED MANY GENTILES TO UNDERSTAND THE GOSPEL OF JESUS CHRIST, AND TO ACCEPT HIM AS THEIR SAVIOR. DARE WE SAY THAT THE HOLY SPIRIT WAS WRONG?

ALL EYES TURN TOWARD JAMES, THE BROTHER OF JESUS, AND LEADER OF THE JERUSALEM CHURCH.

Second Journey

FROM ACTS 15: 13—16: 8

THE JERUSALEM COUNCIL FACES A PROBLEM THAT IS DIVIDING THE CHURCH: MUST GENTILES BECOME JEWS AND OBEY ALL THEIR RULES BEFORE THEY CAN BECOME CHRISTIANS? THE ARGUMENTS ARE PRESENTED. THE COUNCIL TURNS TO JAMES, BROTHER OF JESUS AND HEAD OF THE COUNCIL.

BROTHERS, LET US NOT MAKE IT HARD FOR GENTILES TO BECOME CHRISTIANS. WE SHOULD ASK ONLY THAT THEY OBEY A FEW NECESSARY RULES. THEY MUST AVOID EATING FOOD THAT HAS BEEN OFFERED TO IDOLS, AND THEY MUST LEAD PURE LIVES.

THE COUNCIL AGREES, AND TWO OF ITS MEMBERS, JUDAS BARSABAS AND SILAS, JOIN PAUL AND BARNABAS IN TAKING THE DECISION TO ANTIOCH.

THE NEWS IS RECEIVED WITH JOY IN ANTIOCH THAT JEWS AND GENTILES CAN GO ON WORKING TOGETHER FOR JESUS. WITH THIS SETTLED, PAUL IS FREE TO CONTINUE HIS MISSIONARY WORK IN GENTILE COUNTRIES.

BARNABAS, LET'S MAKE A TRIP TO VISIT THE CHURCHES WE STARTED.

GOOD IDEA-- I'D LIKE TO ASK MARK TO GO WITH US AGAIN.

NO-- MARK LEFT US BEFORE.

I KNOW, BUT WE SHOULD GIVE HIM ANOTHER CHANCE.

PAUL DISAGREES, SO BARNABAS TAKES MARK AND SAILS TO THE ISLAND OF CYPRUS. PAUL TAKES SILAS WITH HIM BY LAND TO VISIT THE CHURCHES HE STARTED.

IN LYSTRA, THE CITY IN WHICH HE HAD BEEN STONED, PAUL FINDS A GROWING CHURCH.

PAUL, I WANT YOU TO MEET TIMOTHY. HE'S BECOME ONE OF OUR BEST YOUNG LEADERS.

I'VE HEARD MANY FINE REPORTS OF YOU, TIMOTHY. WOULD YOU LIKE TO GO WITH SILAS AND ME?

87

Call from Across the Sea

FROM ACTS 16: 9-19

PAUL AND HIS COMPANIONS, SILAS, TIMOTHY, AND DR. LUKE ARE DIRECTED BY THE HOLY SPIRIT TO TROAS. THERE THEY AWAIT FURTHER ORDERS. ONE NIGHT PAUL HAS A VISION.

COME OVER TO MACEDONIA AND HELP US!

EARLY THE NEXT MORNING...

GOD HAS CALLED US TO TAKE THE GOOD NEWS OF JESUS TO MACEDONIA!

WONDERFUL! I'LL ARRANGE PASSAGE ON THE FIRST BOAT SAILING NORTHWEST.

89

90

Earthquake

FROM ACTS 16: 20-37

PAUL RESTORES TO HER RIGHT MIND A GIRL WHO WAS A FORTUNETELLER FOR SOME GREEDY MEN. ANGRY BECAUSE THEIR BUSINESS HAS BEEN RUINED, THE MEN DRAG PAUL AND SILAS BEFORE THE JUDGES IN THE PUBLIC SQUARE. A CROWD GATHERS.

THESE MEN ARE JEWS. THEY ARE TRYING TO MAKE TROUBLE BY TEACHING THINGS AGAINST ROMAN LAW.

YES! WE ALL HEARD HIM!

BUT I--

SILENCE! THERE'LL BE NO TROUBLE IN THIS CITY. GIVE THESE MEN A BEATING AND THROW THEM IN JAIL, AND SEE THAT THEY DON'T ESCAPE.

AFTER A SEVERE BEATING, PAUL AND SILAS ARE TAKEN TO PRISON AND PUT IN STOCKS.

YOU'LL PAY WITH YOUR LIFE IF THESE MEN ESCAPE.

IN SPITE OF THEIR SUFFERING, THE CHRISTIAN MISSIONARIES PRAY AND SING THEIR PRAISES TO GOD.

SUDDENLY— AT MIDNIGHT— THE PRISON FOUNDATION TREMBLES. THE WALLS TWIST AND CRACK-- SNAPPING CHAINS AND HINGES FROM THE HEAVY DOORS.

EARTHQUAKE!

WHEN THE QUAKE IS OVER THE JAILER RUSHES DOWN INTO THE DUNGEON, AFRAID THAT HIS PRISONERS HAVE ESCAPED.

THEY'RE GONE! I MIGHT AS WELL KILL MYSELF.

NO! NO! WE'RE ALL HERE!

BELIEVING THAT PAUL AND SILAS HAD SOMETHING TO DO WITH THE EARTHQUAKE, THE JAILER FALLS ON HIS KNEES BEFORE THEM.

WHAT MUST I DO TO BE SAVED?

BELIEVE ON THE LORD JESUS CHRIST.

THE JAILER QUICKLY TAKES THE TWO PRISONERS TO HIS HOUSE AND TREATS THEIR WOUNDED BODIES. HE AND HIS FAMILY LISTEN EAGERLY AS PAUL TELLS THEM ABOUT JESUS -- AND ALL ARE BAPTIZED.

EARLY IN THE MORNING ROMAN OFFICERS COME TO THE PRISON.

THE JUDGES HAVE ORDERED YOUR RELEASE.

WE ARE ROMAN CITIZENS, YET WE HAD NO TRIAL. NOW THE JUDGES THINK THEY CAN GET RID OF US QUIETLY. TELL THE JUDGES THEMSELVES TO COME AND MAKE OUR RELEASE AS PUBLIC AS OUR BEATING.

Out of Trouble...Into Trouble

FROM ACTS 16: 38—17: 13

THE ROMAN JUDGES, WHO ORDERED PAUL AND SILAS RELEASED FROM PRISON, ARE SURPRISED WHEN THE OFFICER RETURNS WITH A MESSAGE FROM THE PRISONERS.

THOSE MEN ARE ROMAN CITIZENS. THEY DEMAND THAT YOU COME TO THE PRISON AND RELEASE THEM AS PUBLICLY AS YOU PUNISHED THEM.

ROMAN CITIZENS? AND WE SENTENCED THEM WITHOUT A TRIAL! THIS COULD MEAN TROUBLE FOR US.

FORGETTING THEIR DIGNITY THE JUDGES GO IMMEDIATELY TO THE PRISON.

WE ARE TRULY SORRY FOR THE WAY WE TREATED YOU. NOW PLEASE LEAVE THE CITY TO AVOID FURTHER TROUBLE.

WE FORGIVE YOU-- AND WE WILL LEAVE TODAY.

AT THE HOUSE OF LYDIA, PAUL, SILAS, AND TIMOTHY BID THEIR FRIENDS GOOD-BYE.

THANK YOU FOR LEAVING DR. LUKE HERE TO LEAD OUR CHURCH.

WE WILL RETURN SOMEDAY. HOLD FAST TO YOUR FAITH IN JESUS AND HELP OTHERS TO KNOW HIM.

TRAVELING ON SOME 90 MILES, THE MISSIONARIES REACH THESSALONICA ON THE AEGEAN SEA. PAUL GOES AT ONCE TO THE SYNAGOGUE TO PREACH.

THE SCRIPTURES PROMISED THAT A SAVIOR WOULD COME. JESUS, WHO DIED ON THE CROSS AND ROSE FROM THE DEAD, IS THAT SAVIOR.

MANY PEOPLE LISTEN AND BELIEVE -- BUT SOME OF THE JEWISH LEADERS DO NOT.

WE'VE GOT TO GET RID OF HIM BEFORE HE HAS THE WHOLE CITY BELIEVING WHAT HE SAYS.

HE'S STAYING AT JASON'S HOUSE. LET'S GET HIM THERE.

GATHERING A STRONG-ARMED MOB, THE JEWISH LEADERS CALL ON JASON.

IF YOU'RE LOOKING FOR PAUL, HE'S NOT HERE.

YOU'RE HIDING HIM. IF YOU WON'T LET US HAVE HIM, WE'LL TAKE YOU.

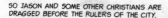
SO JASON AND SOME OTHER CHRISTIANS ARE DRAGGED BEFORE THE RULERS OF THE CITY.

PAUL PREACHES THAT JESUS -- NOT CAESAR -- IS HIS KING. HE'S A TRAITOR,' AND JASON IS PROTECTING HIM.

JASON, YOU AND YOUR FRIENDS WILL HAVE TO DEPOSIT MONEY TO SHOW THAT YOU WILL KEEP THE PEACE. IF THERE'S MORE TROUBLE, YOU WILL LOSE THE MONEY.

To AVOID MAKING TROUBLE FOR THEIR FRIENDS, PAUL AND SILAS LEAVE. FORTY MILES AWAY, IN A HEAVILY FORESTED AREA, THEY REACH BEREA. THERE THE JEWS LISTEN EAGERLY TO PAUL'S PREACHING. EVERY DAY THEY STUDY THE SCRIPTURES. MANY OF THEM BELIEVE -- AND A STRONG CHURCH IS FORMED.

BUT -- UNKNOWN TO PAUL -- MEN FROM THESSALONICA SOON FOLLOW HIM ALONG THE FOREST ROAD...

96

Paul Explains the "Unknown God"

FROM ACTS 17: 13—18: 12; I AND II THESSALONIANS

To escape their enemies in Thessalonica, Paul and his companions, Silas and Timothy, go on to Berea. But unknown to Paul, his enemies follow him.

WE'VE COME TO WARN YOU ABOUT A JEW NAMED PAUL. HE'S A TROUBLEMAKER! DRIVE HIM OUT OF THE CITY AS WE DID.

WE'LL GET RID OF HIM RIGHT NOW!

BUT BEFORE THE ANGRY MOB CAN FIND PAUL, HIS FRIENDS HELP HIM ESCAPE TO ATHENS. FROM THERE PAUL SENDS WORD FOR SILAS AND TIMOTHY TO FOLLOW AS SOON AS POSSIBLE.

IN THE GREAT GREEK CITY—

IDOLS! IDOLS EVERYWHERE! EVEN AN ALTAR TO AN "UNKNOWN GOD."

TO AN UNKNOWN GOD

ON THE SABBATH PAUL PREACHES TO THE JEWS, BUT DURING THE WEEK HE CARRIES HIS MESSAGE OF JESUS TO THE GREEKS IN THE MARKET PLACE.

HE SAYS THERE IS ONLY ONE GOD, AND THAT HE SENT HIS ONLY SON, JESUS, TO HELP US.

I'D LIKE TO HEAR MORE ABOUT A GOD WHO CARES FOR PEOPLE. LET'S ASK THIS MAN TO SPEAK BEFORE THE COURT OF MARS' HILL.

PAUL ACCEPTS THE INVITATION EAGERLY.

GENTLEMEN OF ATHENS, SINCE YOU WORSHIP A GOD YOU DO NOT KNOW, I'LL TELL YOU WHO HE IS-- THE TRUE GOD, WHO MADE ALL THINGS. HE DOES NOT LIVE IN TEMPLES MADE BY HUMAN HANDS. HE IS NOT FAR FROM EACH ONE OF US, FOR IN HIM WE LIVE, AND MOVE, AND HAVE OUR BEING.

THE MEN OF ATHENS LISTEN EAGERLY-- UNTIL PAUL SAYS THAT JESUS ROSE FROM THE DEAD.

NOBODY CAN BE RAISED FROM THE DEAD. WHAT A SILLY IDEA!

I'M NOT SO SURE...

99

IT IS DOING WELL, BUT THE PEOPLE ARE HAVING A HARD TIME.

I'LL WRITE TO THEM AT ONCE.

PAUL'S **First Letter to the Thessalonians**, WHICH IS A BOOK OF THE NEW TESTAMENT.

To the church of the Thessalonians-- from Paul, Silas, and Timothy

We remember how joyfully you turned from idols to serve the true God. Though we had to leave, it was good to receive news that you are standing true to your faith, even though people have been making it hard for you.

As we urged you when we were with you, live in the way that will please God, who invited you to have a place in His Kingdom. Keep on praying, and love one another more and more. I know you have worried about Christians who have died, but you need not. For Jesus promised that when He comes back from Heaven these will meet Him.

Be sure this letter is read to all the members of the church.

PAUL GETS FURTHER WORD FROM HIS FRIENDS IN THESSALONICA. HE WRITES A **Second Letter to the Thessalonians.** THIS ALSO IS A BOOK OF THE NEW TESTAMENT.

To the church of the Thessalonians-- from Paul, Silas, and Timothy

Don't get a mistaken idea of what I told you. No one should quit working because he thinks Jesus will return right away. If anyone will not work, he should not be fed. Before Jesus comes, there will be a time when an evil man tries to rule the world, taking the place of God. But God will keep you from evil. Don't get discouraged in doing what is right.

In any letter that I send to you, I write a few words at the close in my own handwriting-- like this-- so that you will be sure the letter is from me. May Christ's love be with you all.

FOR A YEAR AND A HALF PAUL PREACHES IN CORINTH. A STRONG CHRISTIAN CHURCH IS STARTED. BUT THE JEWISH LEADERS ARE ANGRY AT PAUL AND LOOK UPON HIM AS A TRAITOR TO HIS RELIGION.

GALLIO IS A NEW GOVERNOR. HE WON'T RISK HAVING TROUBLE BREAK OUT RIGHT AWAY. I THINK WE CAN WORK THINGS SO THAT HE WILL GET RID OF PAUL FOR US!

Talk of the Town

FROM ACTS 18: 13—19: 16

Jewish leaders in Corinth are angry because Paul is winning so many people to Jesus. They take him before the new Roman governor.

MOST EXCELLENT GALLIO-- THIS MAN IS TELLING PEOPLE TO WORSHIP GOD IN WAYS THAT ARE AGAINST THE LAW. HE IS CHANGING THE JEWISH CUSTOMS WHICH THE ROMANS PERMIT.

Paul is about to defend himself, but to everyone's surprise Gallio turns on Paul's enemies.

I WILL TAKE NO PART IN QUARRELS ABOUT THE JEWISH RELIGION. THIS HAS NOTHING TO DO WITH ROMAN LAW. NOW, GET OUT OF COURT!

MAP OF PAUL'S WORK IN GREEK CITIES

PHILIPPI
NEAPOLIS
BEREA
THESSALONICA
TROAS
ASIA
ANTIOCH
ICONIUM
LYSTRA
EPHESUS
DERBE
TARSUS
ATHENS
ANTIOCH
CORINTH
MILETUS
SELEUCIA
Mediterranean Sea
CYPRUS
CRETE
SIDON
TYRE
CAESAREA
JERUSALEM

AFTER THIS ORDER BY THE GOVERNOR, PAUL PREACHES IN CORINTH WITHOUT FURTHER TROUBLE-- AND THE CHURCH GROWS. PAUL DECIDES TO GO BACK TO PALESTINE. AQUILA AND PRISCILLA GO WITH HIM AS FAR AS EPHESUS.

PAUL VISITS JERUSALEM-AND ANTIOCH, THEN BEGINS HIS THIRD MISSIONARY JOURNEY. RETURNING TO EPHESUS, HE SEES THE GREAT TEMPLE OF THE GODDESS DIANA WHICH COVERS ACRES OF LAND AND IS CONNECTED TO THE CITY BY A MARBLE HIGHWAY.

LIKE THE PEOPLE OF ATHENS, THE EPHESIANS WORSHIP A GODDESS MADE WITH THEIR OWN HANDS. O GOD, HELP ME TO TEACH THEM THE TRUTH.

IN THE TENTSHOP OF AQUILA AND PRISCILLA GOOD NEWS AWAITS PAUL.

WHILE YOU WERE GONE A MAN NAMED APOLLOS, FROM ALEXANDRIA, CAME HERE. HE KNEW ONLY THE TEACHINGS OF JOHN THE BAPTIST. ALTHOUGH HE'S A GREAT PREACHER, WE EXPLAINED TO HIM MANY THINGS YOU TOLD US ABOUT CHRIST.

HE'S IN CORINTH NOW-- WORKING IN THE CHURCH THERE.

IF ONLY ALL CHRISTIANS WERE MISSIONARIES LIKE YOU.

PAUL BEGINS AT ONCE TO PREACH IN THE SYNAGOGUE, BUT SOME OF THE JEWISH LEADERS START TROUBLE, SO PAUL MOVES INTO A GREEK SCHOOL.

PEOPLE COME FROM MILES AROUND TO HEAR PAUL.

EVERYONE'S TALKING ABOUT THE WAY HE HEALS THE SICK. TRULY HE IS A MAN OF GOD-- DOING GOD'S WORK.

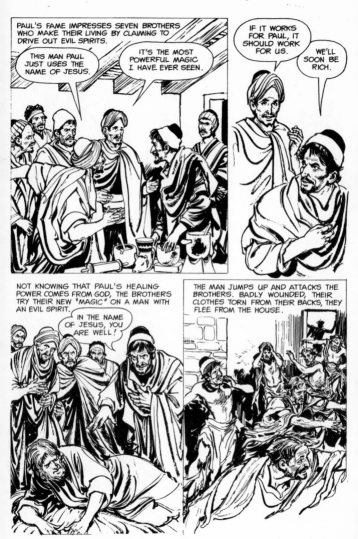

104

The Angry Mob

FROM ACTS 19: 17-30; I CORINTHIANS

THE PEOPLE OF EPHESUS SEE THAT WHAT PAUL SAYS IS TRUE AND THAT THE MAGICIANS ARE FAKES. MANY PERSONS BELIEVE IN CHRIST AND BURN THEIR BOOKS OF MAGIC.

PAUL IS STILL REJOICING WITH THE GROWTH OF THE CHURCH IN EPHESUS WHEN NEWS COMES FROM CORINTH...

PAUL DICTATES A LETTER TO THE CHURCH OF CORINTH, KNOWN AS I Corinthians, IT IS A BOOK OF THE NEW TESTAMENT.

> THE CHURCH IN CORINTH IS HAVING ALL SORTS OF TROUBLES. THE MEMBERS ARE TAKING SIDES AGAINST ONE ANOTHER. SOME OF THEM SAY YOU ARE THE HEAD OF OUR CHURCH. OTHERS SAY APOLLOS IS THE BEST PREACHER -- AND STILL OTHERS SAY PETER IS THE REAL LEADER CHOSEN BY JESUS.

Paul, to the church at Corinth...

I beg of you, my brothers, do not quarrel and divide the church. There is only one head of the Christian Church -- Christ! It was Christ -- not Paul or Apollos or Peter -- who died for you on the cross.

Keep yourselves pure. Don't you see that you yourselves are the temple of God -- and that God's Spirit lives in you? God will destroy anyone who defiles his temple, for his temple is holy -- and that is what you are!

If I knew everything and could speak like an angel but did not have Christian love, I would amount to nothing. Be kind and love one another in the church. I send my love to all of you.

THE CHURCH IN EPHESUS GROWS — ALMOST AS RAPIDLY AS THE BLAZE WHICH DESTROYED THE BOOKS OF MAGIC. IT HAS ITS EFFECT ON THE IDOL MERCHANTS OF THE CITY...

> BUSINESS IS NO GOOD. PEOPLE AREN'T BUYING SILVER TEMPLES OF DIANA.

> IT'S BECAUSE OF THAT CHRISTIAN PREACHER, PAUL. HE IS LEADING THE PEOPLE TO BELIEVE IN JESUS.

107

THE CROWD GROWS AS IT PUSHES THROUGH THE STREETS -- SOON THE WHOLE CITY IS IN AN UPROAR...

GREAT IS DIANA OF THE EPHESIANS!

AND THE MOB TAKES PAUL'S FRIENDS TO THE GREAT OUTDOOR THEATER.

A FEW MINUTES LATER IN ANOTHER PART OF THE CITY...

PAUL! THE SILVERSMITHS ARE AFTER YOU FOR DESTROYING THEIR BUSINESS. THEY HAVE SEIZED GAIUS AND ARISTARCHUS AND...

WHERE ARE THEY?

NO! PAUL! THAT MOB WILL KILL YOU!

108

Riot in Ephesus

FROM ACTS 19: 31—20: 3; ROMANS; II CORINTHIANS

CITY OFFICIALS BEG PAUL TO STAY AWAY FROM THE MOB. FOR TWO HOURS THE RIOTERS SHOUT, "GREAT IS DIANA OF THE EPHESIANS." FINALLY THE TOWN CLERK MAKES HIMSELF HEARD...

GENTLEMEN OF EPHESUS -- IF THE SILVERSMITHS HAVE A COMPLAINT, LET THEM BRING IT BEFORE THE COURTS. I WARN YOU -- IF THE ROMAN GOVERNMENT ASKS THE REASON FOR THIS RIOTING, THERE IS NO EXCUSE WE CAN GIVE FOR IT.

IN FACE OF THIS THREAT, THE RIOT BREAKS UP. PAUL SENDS FOR HIS FRIENDS.

THE MOB WAS REALLY AFTER ME-- SO TO PREVENT TROUBLE FOR ALL OF YOU, I WILL GO TO PHILIPPI.

OUR PRAYERS WILL GO WITH YOU.

SOON AFTER PAUL REACHES PHILIPPI, TITUS JOINS HIM WITH NEWS FROM CORINTH.

PAUL, YOUR LETTER TO THE CHRISTIANS AT CORINTH MADE THEM CORRECT THEIR WRONG-DOING. BUT NOW SOME PEOPLE HAVE COME TO CORINTH WHO CLAIM YOU ARE NOT A TRUE APOSTLE OF JESUS.

ONCE AGAIN PAUL WRITES TO THE CHURCH IN CORINTH. THE LETTER--KNOWN AS II *Corinthians*--IS A BOOK OF THE NEW TESTAMENT.

I can see that my letter upset you, but I am glad I sent it. Not because I want to hurt you, but to make you sorry as God would have you sorry for the things that were wrong.

We are taking a collection for poor Christians in Jerusalem. Other churches have given large sums. I trust you will be able to do the same. Let everyone give what he has decided in his own heart to give, for God loves a cheerful giver.

And now, for those who question whether or not I am a true minister of Christ. I have been imprisoned, I have been beaten many times, I have often faced death. I have been stoned, I have been shipwrecked three times--all to carry out the work of Christ. When I visit you again, I hope it will be a happy meeting. Good-bye till then.

WHILE TITUS TAKES THE LETTER TO CORINTH, PAUL CONTINUES VISITING CHURCHES IN MACEDONIA, COLLECTING MONEY FOR THE POOR IN JERUSALEM. MONTHS LATER HE REACHES CORINTH WHERE HE IS GREETED BY FRIENDS WHO HAVE GIVEN EAGERLY TO HIS COLLECTION.

THIS MONEY WILL SHOW THE CHRISTIANS IN JERUSALEM THAT YOU'RE CONCERNED FOR THEM.

110

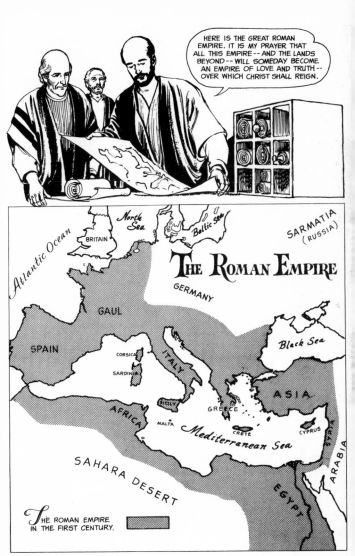

111

To carry out this dream, and to prepare for a visit to Rome, Paul writes to the Christians in that city. His letter, called **Romans**, is a book of the New Testament.

Greetings from Paul to the Christians in Rome. When I go on a new missionary journey, I would like to stop awhile with you.

I am not ashamed to preach the Gospel, for the message of Christ is powerful. People of every part of the world are sinners. All need the salvation God provided by sending His Son to die in our place so that we might be forgiven. Those who believe are changed in their whole way of living.

Give yourselves entirely to God and let your actions be such as will please Him. Please pray for me, that I may be kept safe from danger. God be with you all.

After finishing his work in Corinth, Paul prepares to go to Jerusalem for the great Passover feast. But his enemies learn of his plans.

LET HIM GO-- A SHIP AT SEA WILL BE JUST THE PLACE FOR OUR MEN TO GET RID OF HIM.

WITH PAUL OUT OF THE WAY, WE'LL GET THE PEOPLE TO GIVE UP THEIR CHRISTIAN RELIGION.

On a beautiful spring morning a ship makes ready to sail from the harbor of Corinth...

LOOK AT ALL THOSE PEOPLE GOING TO JERUSALEM.

I KNOW ONE MAN WHO WILL NEVER REACH THAT CITY!

Bound—Hand and Foot

FROM ACTS 20: 3—21: 14

115

PAUL GOES ON TO TYRE, WHERE HE PREACHES FOR A WEEK. WHEN HE LEAVES, THE CHRISTIANS FOLLOW HIM TO THE BEACH FOR A PRAYERFUL GOOD-BY.

DON'T GO TO JERUSALEM. JEWS ARE THERE WAITING TO KILL YOU BECAUSE YOU SAY JESUS IS THE SON OF GOD.

I MUST GO. I HAVE MONEY WHICH GENTILE CHRISTIANS HAVE GIVEN ME FOR THE POOR IN JERUSALEM. I AM NOT AFRAID...

FARTHER DOWN THE COAST AT CAESAREA, PAUL VISITS WITH PHILIP THE EVANGELIST. THE PROPHET AGABUS JOINS THEM, AND--SUDDENLY-- WHILE THEY ARE TALKING HE TAKES PAUL'S BELT AND BEGINS TO BIND HIS OWN HANDS AND FEET.

WHAT DOES THIS MEAN?

THE HOLY SPIRIT TELLS ME THAT THE MAN TO WHOM THE BELT BELONGS WILL BE BOUND-- LIKE THIS-- BY THE JEWS IN JERUSALEM AND HANDED OVER TO THE GENTILES.

PAUL-- GIVE UP YOUR PLANS TO GO TO JERUSALEM. FOR OUR SAKE--

WHY DO YOU TRY TO WEAKEN ME WITH YOUR TEARS? I AM PREPARED NOT ONLY TO BE BOUND, BUT TO DIE FOR THE SAKE OF THE LORD JESUS.

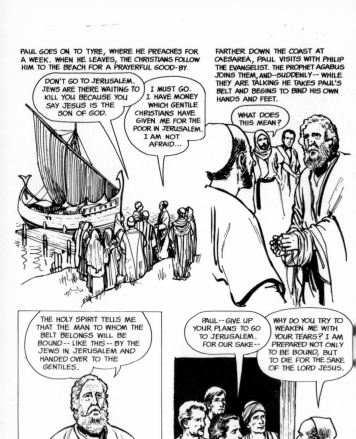

A Boy and a Secret

FROM ACTS 21: 15—23: 24

THE DAY AFTER PAUL REACHES JERUSALEM, HE MEETS WITH JAMES AND OTHER LEADERS OF THE JERUSALEM CHURCH. HE DELIVERS THE MONEY FOR THE POOR AND TELLS WHAT GOD HAS DONE IN OTHER LANDS.

I MUST WARN YOU, PAUL, YOU HAVE ENEMIES HERE WHO THINK YOU ARE A TRAITOR. EVEN THE CHRISTIAN JEWS HAVE QUESTIONS BECAUSE OF YOUR WORK AMONG THE GENTILES.

I'LL WORSHIP WITH THEM IN THE TEMPLE TO SHOW THAT I AM TRUE TO THE FAITH OF OUR FATHERS.

JAMES' WARNING COMES TRUE WITHIN THE WEEK. WHILE PAUL IS WORSHIPING IN THE TEMPLE HIS ENEMIES ACCUSE HIM, FALSELY, OF BRINGING GENTILES INTO GOD'S HOUSE WHERE ONLY JEWS ARE ALLOWED.

THERE HE IS -- THE TRAITOR!

HE HAS DEFILED THIS HOLY PLACE OF GOD!

118

BUT PAUL'S ENEMIES WILL NOT GIVE UP. THE NEXT MORNING...

WE'LL ASK THE COMMANDING OFFICER TO BRING PAUL BEFORE THE COURT AGAIN FOR QUESTIONING. WHILE PAUL IS ON THE WAY, WE WILL KILL HIM!

AND NOT ONE OF US WILL EAT OR DRINK UNTIL THE TRAITOR IS DEAD!

IN THEIR EAGERNESS THE PLOTTERS TALK TOO FREELY, AND A BOY LEARNS OF THE PLOT. HE RACES TO THE PRISON.

UNCLE PAUL, YOUR ENEMIES ARE WAITING TO KILL YOU. I HEARD THEIR PLAN--

PAUL ASKS AN OFFICER TO TAKE THE BOY TO THE COMMANDING OFFICER, WHO LISTENS TO THE STORY AND THEN SENDS THE BOY HOME.

THERE'LL BE NO MORE TROUBLE IN JERUSALEM. GET READY A GUARD OF 200 SOLDIERS, 70 HORSEMEN, AND 200 SPEARMEN. TAKE PAUL TO CAESAREA --AND LEAVE BY NINE O'CLOCK TONIGHT!

Paul Pleads His Case

FROM ACTS 23: 25—28: 4

TO PROTECT PAUL'S LIFE, THE ROMAN COMMANDER AT JERUSALEM SENDS HIM TO CAESAREA, WHERE PAUL IS KEPT IN PRISON. AFTER TWO YEARS PAUL APPEARS BEFORE FESTUS, THE ROMAN GOVERNOR, AND DEMANDS HIS RIGHT TO BE TRIED BY THE EMPEROR NERO AT ROME. BUT FIRST FESTUS BRINGS PAUL BEFORE A NEIGHBORING RULER, KING AGRIPPA, WHO IS VISITING THE CITY.

I ONCE THOUGHT IT MY DUTY TO OPPOSE JESUS. I HAD MANY OF HIS FOLLOWERS IMPRISONED. BUT ON MY WAY TO DAMASCUS I SAW A LIGHT FROM HEAVEN... AND JESUS SAID TO ME, "I SEND YOU TO TURN PEOPLE OF ALL NATIONS FROM THE POWER OF SATAN TO GOD... O KING AGRIPPA, I COULD NOT DISOBEY THE HEAVENLY VISION.

YOU'RE TRYING TO PERSUADE ME TO BE A CHRISTIAN.

FESTUS AND AGRIPPA WOULD HAVE SET PAUL FREE IF HE HAD NOT DEMANDED A TRIAL IN ROME. SO--UNDER ROMAN GUARD AND ACCOMPANIED BY LUKE-- PAUL IS TAKEN ABOARD A SHIP BOUND FOR ROME. AT THE ISLAND OF CRETE...

THE WINTER STORMS WILL SOON BE HERE. IT WILL BE DANGEROUS TO GO ON UNTIL SPRING.

THE HARBOR AT PHOENIX IS NOT FAR AWAY--WE'LL SPEND THE WINTER THERE.

THE SHIP SETS SAIL--ONLY TO BE STRUCK BY A RAGING "NORTHEASTER."

TAKE DOWN THE MAINSAIL!

ON THE 14TH NIGHT OF THE STORM THE SAILORS TRY TO DESERT THE SHIP.

UNLESS THOSE MEN STAY WITH THE SHIP, YOU CANNOT BE SAVED!

THE SOLDIERS CUT THE SMALL BOAT LOOSE --AND THE SAILORS ARE FORCED TO STAY WITH THE SHIP. AT DAYBREAK...

LAND AHEAD!

HEADING TOWARD A BAY, THE SHIP RUNS AGROUND. THE BOW STICKS FAST, BUT THE STERN BEGINS TO BREAK UNDER THE POUNDING OF THE HEAVY WAVES.

ABANDON SHIP!

KILL THE PRISONERS-- IF THEY REACH SHORE THEY'LL ESCAPE.

BECAUSE OF HIS FRIENDSHIP FOR PAUL, THE ROMAN OFFICER SPARES THE PRISONERS. SOLDIERS, SAILORS, PASSENGERS, AND PRISONERS STRUGGLE FOR THEIR LIVES IN THE RAGING SEA.

IN ANSWER TO PAUL'S PRAYERS, ALL 276 MEN ON BOARD REACH LAND SAFELY. PEOPLE ON THE ISLAND OF MALTA RUSH DOWN TO THE SHORE TO HELP THE VICTIMS OF THE WRECK.

I'LL GET SOME MORE WOOD.

WE'LL HAVE A FIRE GOING SOON.

AS PAUL LAYS SOME STICKS ON THE FIRE A SNAKE CRAWLS OUT OF THE BUNDLE-- AND STRIKES!

A VIPER!

THE MAN ACTS AS IF HE DOESN'T KNOW THAT A VIPER'S BITE MEANS AGONY AND DEATH!

HE MUST BE A MURDERER! HE ESCAPED THE SEA -- BUT JUSTICE WILL NOT LET HIM LIVE.

Prisoner in Rome
FROM ACTS 28: 5-31; PHILEMON; COLOSSIANS; EPHESIANS

A PRISONER ON HIS WAY TO ROME, PAUL IS SHIPWRECKED WITH THE WHOLE CREW ON THE ISLAND OF MALTA. HE IS BITTEN BY A SNAKE AND THE PEOPLE OF MALTA EXPECT TO SEE HIM FALL DEAD. BUT AFTER A TIME...

ANY OTHER MAN WOULD HAVE DIED BY THIS TIME!

HE MUST BE A GOD!

THE NEWS OF THIS MIRACLE SPREADS -- AND PAUL IS INVITED TO THE GOVERNOR'S HOUSE. THE GOVERNOR TELLS PAUL ABOUT HIS FATHER.

HE IS VERY ILL, AND I AM AFRAID HE WILL NOT RECOVER.

LET ME SEE HIM. I WILL ASK GOD TO HEAL HIM.

AFTER ASKING GOD'S HELP, PAUL PRAYS FOR THE SICK MAN -- AND HE IS MADE WELL.

SOON, MANY OF THE PEOPLE ON THE ISLAND COME BEGGING FOR HELP. PAUL PRAYS FOR THEM, AND SPENDS THE WINTER PREACHING.

IN THE SPRING, THE SHIPWRECKED GROUP SAILS ON ANOTHER SHIP TO ITALY. STILL UNDER GUARD, PAUL WALKS DOWN THE GREAT APPIAN WAY TOWARD ROME.

I HOPE YOU ARE FOUND INNOCENT AT YOUR TRIAL.

THANK YOU. I AM GUILTY ONLY OF PREACHING THE TRUTH: JESUS IS THE SON OF GOD!

AT THE FORUM OF APPIUS...

PAUL! WE'RE CHRISTIANS FROM ROME. WE'VE COME TO WALK BACK TO ROME WITH YOU.

THEY'VE WALKED 40 MILES JUST TO GREET HIM! HOW THESE CHRISTIANS LOVE HIM!

IN ROME PAUL LIVES IN A PRIVATE HOUSE AWAITING TRIAL. THOUGH CHAINED TO A GUARD, HE CAN HAVE VISITORS. PAUL TELLS EACH OF THEM ABOUT CHRIST.

COME BACK. BRING YOUR FRIENDS -- JEWS AS WELL AS ROMANS!

WE WILL -- WE WANT TO LEARN MORE!

126

ONE MAN WHO BELIEVES IN JESUS IS ONESIMUS. HE BECOMES PAUL'S FAITHFUL FRIEND AND SERVANT. AND ONE DAY PAUL TELLS HIM...

ONESIMUS, YOU ARE LIKE A SON TO ME.

FORGIVE ME FOR NOT TELLING YOU-- I AM A SLAVE; WHEN I RAN AWAY FROM COLOSSE, I ROBBED MY MASTER, PHILEMON.

PHILEMON OF COLOSSE? WHY, HE'S A FRIEND OF MINE -- AND A CHRISTIAN. YOU SHOULD NOT HAVE LEFT SUCH A GOOD MAN.

SEVERAL DAYS LATER ...

I WISH I COULD KEEP YOU WITH ME, ONESIMUS, BUT IT IS RIGHT THAT YOU SHOULD GO BACK TO PHILEMON. HE IS YOUR MASTER.

YES, I MUST ASK HIS FORGIVENESS-- NO MATTER HOW HE CHOOSES TO PUNISH ME.

FOR ONESIMUS' SAKE PAUL WRITES A LETTER TO Philemon. THE LETTER IS A BOOK OF THE NEW TESTAMENT.

I thank God for you, Philemon, for I know that you love Jesus and all His followers. I ask you to forgive Onesimus. He did not live up to his name, which means "useful," but he is useful to both of us now. You lost a slave; you are getting back a Christian brother. If he owes you anything, charge it to me. I, Paul, will repay you. I know you will do what I ask-- in fact, I believe you will do even more.

Paul

127

SINCE HE IS SENDING ONESIMUS BACK TO COLOSSE,
PAUL WRITES A LETTER TO THE **Colossians**,
AND ANOTHER TO THE **Ephesians** AND OTHER
CHURCHES IN NEARBY CITIES. THESE LETTERS ARE
BOOKS OF THE NEW TESTAMENT.

To the Christian
brothers at Colosse,

I thank God for the good
things I have heard about
your church. Always remember
that Christ is above every
other power--whether angels
or men. You have salvation
through faith in Him.

Do everything as Christians
should--wives and husbands,
children and parents, servants
and masters. Onesimus will
tell you what is going on
here where I am. Also exchange
this letter with the one I
am sending to the other
churches, and read that
one, too.

To the Christian believers
at Ephesus, or at other places
where this letter is read,

It was God's plan before
He made the world to gather
people of all nations into the
Church, of which Christ is the
Head. The time has come, and
you Gentiles, who were con-
sidered outsiders, have been
brought into the family of God.

Put on God's armor so that
you can stand against the
Devil. Take the belt of truth,
the shield of faith, and the
sword, which is God's Word.
Pray for all Christians, and
for me, a preacher in chains.
May all who love Christ have
the peace that God gives.

SEVERAL MONTHS AFTER ONESIMUS AND
A FELLOW CHRISTIAN LEAVE WITH PAUL'S LETTERS,
ANOTHER TRAVELER REACHES ROME AND KNOCKS
ON THE DOOR OF THE HOUSE WHERE PAUL LIVES.

Apostle on the March

FROM PHILIPPIANS; I TIMOTHY; TITUS

FOR MONTHS PAUL WAITS-- CHAINED TO A ROMAN GUARD-- FOR HIS TRIAL BEFORE THE EMPEROR IN ROME. HIS CHRISTIAN FRIENDS IN ALL THE CHURCHES PRAY FOR HIM CONSTANTLY, AND ONE DAY...

GREETINGS, PAUL, I HAVE COME WITH A GIFT FROM THE CHURCH AT PHILIPPI.

EPAPHRODITUS! WHAT A BLESSING TO HAVE SUCH FRIENDS!

HE TRAVELED OVER 800 MILES JUST TO DELIVER A GIFT!

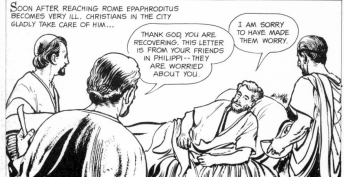

SOON AFTER REACHING ROME EPAPHRODITUS BECOMES VERY ILL. CHRISTIANS IN THE CITY GLADLY TAKE CARE OF HIM...

THANK GOD, YOU ARE RECOVERING. THIS LETTER IS FROM YOUR FRIENDS IN PHILIPPI-- THEY ARE WORRIED ABOUT YOU.

I AM SORRY TO HAVE MADE THEM WORRY.

AS SOON AS HE IS WELL, EPAPHRODITUS GOES TO SEE PAUL.

THE CHURCH IN ROME IS GROWING RAPIDLY. UNLESS YOU NEED ME HERE, I WOULD LIKE TO GO BACK HOME.

YES, THAT'S WHAT YOU SHOULD DO. I HAVE WRITTEN A LETTER TO MY FRIENDS IN PHILIPPI. YOU CAN TAKE IT BACK WITH YOU.

PAUL'S LETTER TO THE **Philippians** IS A BOOK OF THE NEW TESTAMENT.

To the church at Philippi,
I don't know yet how my trial will come out, but I believe God will let me visit you again. Make me happy by living in harmony among yourselves. Think as Christ did. Though divine, He was willing to humble Himself and become a Man--willing even to die on the cross.

Thank you for your gift which Epaphroditus brought. You have been generous. God will also supply all that you need. Always be glad, since you are Christians, and think about the things that are good. The Christians here send greetings, especially the ones who are working in Caesar's palace.

TWO YEARS--AND FINALLY PAUL'S CASE IS BROUGHT TO COURT.* BEFORE NERO, THE MOST POWERFUL RULER IN THE WORLD, PAUL MAKES HIS DEFENSE, AND IN A FEW DAYS...

THANK GOD! NOW I CAN CARRY OUT MY DREAM TO TAKE THE GOSPEL OF CHRIST TO THE FARTHEST CORNERS OF THE EMPIRE!

PAUL! PAUL! THE COURT HAS SET YOU FREE!

*ALTHOUGH THE BIBLE DOES NOT TELL ABOUT PAUL'S RELEASE, THE LETTERS HE WROTE AFTER-WARD SHOW THAT IT MUST HAVE TAKEN PLACE.

I HAVE HOPED THAT I WOULD BE THE ONE ALLOWED TO REMOVE YOUR CHAINS.

THANK YOU -- IT'S GOOD TO BE FREE.

AFTER TWO YEARS IN PRISON PAUL REVISITS MANY OF THE CHURCHES HE HELPED TO START. FOLLOWING A VISIT WITH HIS HELPER, TIMOTHY, IN EPHESUS HE GOES ON TO PHILIPPI. BUT HE CANNOT FORGET THE PROBLEMS TIMOTHY FACES AND HE WRITES HIM A LETTER.

PAUL'S LETTER, KNOWN AS **I Timothy,** IS A BOOK OF THE NEW TESTAMENT.

FROM PHILIPPI, PAUL GOES TO THE ISLAND OF CRETE -- TAKING ANOTHER HELPER, TITUS, WITH HIM. THERE THEY ORGANIZE CHURCHES, BUT AFTER A WHILE...

I asked you to stay at Ephesus to take charge of the church there when I went on to Troas and Philippi. Tell people to stop arguing about foolish questions that do not help them as Christians. See that those who are chosen to be leaders in the church are men of good character and ability.

If you have to correct people, do it in a kindly way, as you would to a member of your own family. Don't let anyone look down on you because you are young. Be a good example, and be faithful in your work as a preacher.

I WISH I HAD MORE TIME TO SPEND HERE, BUT I MUST GO ON. WILL YOU STAY AND HELP THE PEOPLE HERE, TITUS?

I'LL WORK ANY PLACE TO SERVE MY LORD!

TITUS AND HIS PROBLEMS AT CRETE ARE MUCH ON PAUL'S MIND AS HE CONTINUES HIS TRAVELS. HE WRITES TO **Titus** -- THE LETTER BECOMES A BOOK OF THE NEW TESTAMENT...

I left you on the island of Crete to finish organizing the churches there. Choose leaders who are worthy, for there are many who would lead people astray.

The people of Crete are lazy and sinful. One of their own ancient teachers said this. Therefore be strict with them. Teach them to live useful and honest lives so that God's message will not be blamed. Remind them to show respect to rulers, and to be kind -- for God was kind to us when He sent Christ to be our Savior.

Come to me when I send one of my other helpers to take your place.

WHILE PAUL TRAVELS, PREACHES, AND WRITES LETTERS TO SPREAD THE GOSPEL OF CHRIST THROUGHOUT THE GREAT ROMAN EMPIRE, THE PEOPLE OF ROME ARE TURNING AGAINST NERO, THEIR EMPEROR. HIS GREED AND UGLY MANNERS ANGER THEM.

ONE NIGHT WHILE THE CITY SLEEPS...

132

The Burning of Rome

II TIMOTHY

IT IS THE YEAR 64. NERO, THE CRUEL EMPEROR OF ROME, HAS MANY ENEMIES AMONG HIS OWN PEOPLE. THERE ARE RUMORS OF PLOTS AGAINST HIS LIFE. THEN, STRANGELY, A FIRE SWEEPS ACROSS THE CITY. FOR NINE DAYS IT RAGES -- BURNING GREAT SECTIONS OF THE CITY AND DRIVING THOUSANDS FROM THEIR HOMES. FROM HIS PALACE, NERO WATCHES...

EVEN WHILE THE CITY IS STILL IN FLAMES, NEW RUMORS SPREAD.

NERO! THE PEOPLE ARE SAYING **YOU** STARTED THE FIRE. THERE ARE UGLY THREATS--

AND I SAY THE CHRISTIANS STARTED THE FIRE. ARREST THEM-- TORTURE THEM-- KILL THEM!

THIS WILL TURN PEOPLE'S ATTENTION AWAY FROM ME.

ARMED WITH ORDERS FROM THE EMPEROR, SOLDIERS KILL HUNDREDS OF CHRISTIANS IN ROME. THE ORDER REACHES OUT ACROSS THE SEA FROM ITALY-- AND ONCE AGAIN PAUL IS ARRESTED!

BY ORDER OF THE EMPEROR, YOU ARE UNDER ARREST!

ONCE AGAIN PAUL COMES TO ROME--A PRISONER. THIS TIME HE IS CHAINED TO THE WALL OF THE MAMERTINE PRISON. LUKE COMES TO COMFORT HIM.

I'M SURE I HAVE ONLY A FEW MONTHS TO LIVE. BRING SOME PAPER AND A PEN AND WRITE WHAT I TELL YOU TO TIMOTHY.

I'LL BRING THE MATERIAL ON MY NEXT VISIT.

When Luke returns, Paul tells him what to write. The letter, II Timothy, is a book of the New Testament.

When Timothy receives the letter, he sails at once to Rome. There he finds Luke, who takes him to the prison. But as Timothy greets Paul...

I HAVE JUST RECEIVED ORDERS -- YOU ARE UNDER ARREST!

Dear Timothy,

Be strong, like a good soldier for Christ. Remember the truth as you learned from me and from the Holy Scriptures. Keep preaching it, even though the time will come when people don't want to hear the truth.

I want to see you very much. Do your best to come before winter. Bring the coat I left at Troas, and the books. I have almost reached the end of my life. Soon I will be with the Lord and He will give me a place in His heavenly Kingdom. Try to come soon.

Paul

So Timothy, too, is arrested for teaching about Jesus. In their prison cells the two missionaries wait for Roman law to bring them to trial. In time Paul's case is called. Alone, he is marched to the court of Nero.

135

Soldier Victorious

FROM II TIMOTHY 4: 6-8

IN ROME, PAUL IS ON TRIAL FOR HIS LIFE BEFORE THE CRUEL EMPEROR, NERO.

I FIND YOU GUILTY OF STIRRING UP TROUBLE IN THE EMPIRE. THE SENTENCE IS DEATH-- BY THE SWORD.

QUICKLY SOLDIERS TAKE PAUL OUTSIDE THE CITY -- TO BEHEAD HIM.

I HAVE FOUGHT THE GOOD FIGHT. I HAVE FINISHED MY COURSE. I HAVE KEPT THE FAITH.

SO DEATH COMES TO PAUL, WHO FOUNDED CHRISTIAN CHURCHES ON TWO CONTINENTS AND WHO WAS LED BY GOD TO WRITE NEARLY HALF OF THE BOOKS OF THE NEW TESTAMENT.

BUT PAUL'S DEATH DOES NOT BRING A HALT TO THE GOSPEL. CHRIST'S CHURCH MARCHES ON -- THROUGHOUT THE ROMAN EMPIRE, AND THEN ACROSS THE WORLD.

THE END OF AN ERA

FROM HEBREWS THROUGH REVELATION

JESUS' DISCIPLES WHO WERE STILL ALIVE WERE GROWING OLD IN THE LATTER HALF OF THE FIRST CENTURY AFTER HIS BIRTH. THEY COULD NOT TRAVEL TO ALL THE CHURCHES, SO THEY TURNED TO WRITING LETTERS TO JESUS' FOLLOWERS.

THE LAST NINE BOOKS OF THE NEW TESTAMENT, HEBREWS THROUGH REVELATION, ARE MESSAGES THESE MEN WROTE TO GIVE ADVICE, COURAGE, AND COMFORT TO THE EARLY CHRISTIANS.

The Book of Hebrews

THE LETTER TO THE HEBREWS WAS WRITTEN AT A TIME WHEN JEWISH CHRISTIANS WERE BEING PRESSURED BY THE ROMANS AND JEWS TO GIVE UP THEIR FAITH IN JESUS.

THEY ASKED THEMSELVES: WHICH IS RIGHT, FAITH IN JESUS OR FAITH IN THE RELIGION OF OUR FOREFATHERS ABRAHAM, MOSES AND DAVID?

"GOD HAS SPOKEN TO US THROUGH HIS SON, JESUS," THE LETTER SAID. "ABRAHAM, MOSES, AND DAVID WERE GREAT MEN WHO LIVED BY FAITH. THEY DIED; BUT JESUS CHRIST WILL LIVE FOREVER. HOLD FAST TO YOUR FAITH IN HIM."

THE LETTER ALSO BROUGHT THE GOOD NEWS THAT TIMOTHY HAD BEEN RELEASED FROM PRISON.

The Book of James

AS LEADER OF THE CHURCH IN JERUSALEM, JAMES, THE BROTHER OF JESUS, WROTE A LETTER OF ADVICE TO CHRISTIANS LIVING IN OTHER COUNTRIES.

"True religion is shown by what you do. Help those who need help. Be fair to all people. Ask God for wisdom, and keep your lives pure."

THUS THE BROTHER OF JESUS, WHO WAS KNOWN AS JAMES THE JUST, CONTINUED TO SPREAD THE GOSPEL.

The Book of I Peter

PETER WAS NOW AN OLD MAN. HE COULD SEE THAT THE ROMANS WERE TURNING AGAINST THE CHRISTIANS AND THAT JESUS' FOLLOWERS WOULD BE IN GREAT DANGER. HE HAD SILAS WRITE A LETTER FOR HIM.

"Face your hardships bravely." Peter told the people. "There is one thing no one can take from you -- the hope of living in Heaven with Christ. Trust in Him; He will reward those who follow Him faithfully."

The Book of II Peter

PETER KNEW THAT HE DID NOT HAVE MANY YEARS TO LIVE. HE WANTED TO HELP THE FOLLOWERS OF JESUS TO BE TRUE TO HIM, SO HE SENT THEM THIS LETTER.

"You believe in Jesus," he wrote, "Then act the way His followers should." Then he warned the Christians not to be upset by people who laughed at them because they believed that Jesus would return.

"When the time is right," Peter wrote, "Christ will return.

"God is giving people a chance to repent. He has promised a new world for those who love and obey Him.

"See how important it is for you to live for God!"

THESE ARE THE LAST WORDS WE HEAR FROM THE FISHERMAN WHO GAVE UP HIS NETS TO FOLLOW JESUS.

The Book of I John

JOHN, WHO HAD BEEN SO CLOSE TO JESUS IN EARLIER YEARS, WAS NOW THE LEADER OF THE CHRISTIANS AROUND EPHESUS.

"I have been with Jesus," John wrote to his people, "and I want you to have the same joy in knowing Him that I have. Don't believe anyone who says that God's Son did not come to the world as a real Person. God loved us and sent His Son to be our Savior. As He loved us, we should love one another."

The Book of II John

"I was very glad," John wrote, "to find some of your children living by the truth and obeying God's command to love one another. If any enemies of the truth come to you teaching that Christ was not a real man, do not receive them into your house. If you do, you will be helping in this evil work."

The Book of III John

"Dear Gaius," John wrote to his Christian friend, "I have heard good things about you. You are doing right in receiving Christians into your home, especially traveling preachers. Your kindness helps in their work. Don't pay attention to anyone who tries to stop you from doing this."

The Book of Jude

JUDE, ANOTHER BROTHER OF JESUS, DID NOT BELIEVE THAT JESUS WAS THE SON OF GOD-- UNTIL HE ROSE FROM THE DEAD. THEN JUDE BECAME A CHRISTIAN AND AFTER THAT HE WAS A STRONG WORKER FOR CHRIST.
ONE DAY HE RECEIVED BAD NEWS-- THAT MEN IN SOME OF THE CHURCHES WERE TEACHING THINGS THAT WERE NOT TRUE.

JUDE WROTE THE CHURCHES A LETTER:

"*You must defend our Christian faith. You have been warned that people would try to turn you away from Christ. I understand some of these false teachers are with you now. Pray that God will keep you strong, and that He will help you strengthen others.*"

The Book of Revelation

JOHN, WHO WROTE THE BEST-LOVED GOSPEL AND THREE LETTERS TO THE FOLLOWER OF JESUS, ALSO WROTE THE BOOK OF REVELATION-- TO HELP CHRISTIANS FACE THE ANGRY POWER OF ROME.

THE ROMANS HAD ARRESTED JOHN AND SENT HIM AS A PRISONER TO THE ISLAND OF PATMOS. THERE HE SAW A VISION OF HEAVEN, AND HE HEARD JESUS SAY:

"BEHOLD, I STAND AT THE DOOR, AND KNOCK: IF ANY MAN HEAR MY VOICE, AND OPEN THE DOOR, I WILL COME IN TO HIM."

IN HEAVEN JOHN SAW THE BOOK OF LIFE-- IN WHICH WERE WRITTEN THE NAMES OF THOSE WHO LOVE CHRIST. AND FINALLY, THE OLD DISCIPLE SAW THE HOLY CITY, WHERE THERE IS NO SICKNESS, NO SORROW, NO DEATH. THOSE WHOSE NAMES ARE IN THE BOOK OF LIFE WILL ENTER THE GLORIOUS CITY AND LIVE FOREVER WITH CHRIST!

AND WITH JOHN'S VISION ENDS THE GREATEST STORY EVER TOLD, THE STORY OF THE BIBLE.

THIS PARTICULAR BIBLE WAS BROUGHT FROM ENGLAND IN 1750 BY JOSIAH DANIELS. WHERE THE BIBLE ITSELF CAME FROM IS A MUCH MORE INTERESTING STORY!

DID YOU KNOW, FOR INSTANCE, THAT THE BIBLE WAS THE FIRST BOOK PRINTED AFTER PRINTING WAS INVENTED?

—OR THAT THE WORD "BIBLE" MEANS A COLLECTION OF BOOKS?... A COLLECTION OF *THE* BOOKS.

THE HOLY BIBLE

OUR WHOLE WAY OF LIFE IS BASED ON THINGS THIS BOOK TELLS US. IT'S BEEN GUIDING MEN FOR THOUSANDS OF YEARS!

WHO WROTE THE BIBLE? WHERE DID IT COME FROM?

THE BIBLE COMES FROM GOD, SON. IT WAS WRITTEN LONG AGO BY MANY MEN, ALL INSPIRED BY GOD. ONE SUCH MAN WAS THE PROPHET JEREMIAH...

GOD USED JEREMIAH TO WARN ISRAEL, NOT JUST WITH THE SPOKEN WORD, BUT WITH THE WRITTEN WORD.

THE PEOPLE HAVE TURNED FROM GOD. WRITE THESE WORDS, BARUCH. THEY MUST BE WARNED!

BUT NOT EVERYONE ACCEPTED GOD'S WORDS. THE KING WAS ANGRY.

I AM THE LAW IN THIS LAND! OUR PEOPLE ARE HAPPY WITHOUT THIS JEREMIAH AND HIS PROPHECIES.

BUT JEREMIAH WAS EVEN ANGRIER!

HE CAN'T DESTROY THE WORD OF GOD BY BURNING A SCROLL! BARUCH, WE'LL WRITE THE WORDS AGAIN!

BUT, JEREMIAH, YOUR LIFE WILL BE IN DANGER IF YOU DEFY THE KING.

GOD HAS COMMANDED THAT THIS WARNING REACH THE PEOPLE. WE CAN'T WORRY ABOUT A KING. WRITE THESE WORDS AS I SAY THEM...

NOT ONLY JEREMIAH'S WRITINGS BUT ALL WRITINGS INSPIRED BY GOD WERE CAREFULLY PRESERVED AND COPIED BY HAND...

AS OLD COPIES WORE OUT NEW ONES WERE MADE WITH GREAT CARE.

As new rulers conquered them, the Hebrew people often had to risk their lives to preserve the word of God.

When the new copies were made, worn texts were carefully buried in caves.

Centuries later...copies of scrolls and old books were found. In 1844 a Bible scholor, Count Tischendorf, visits the monastery of St. Catherine near Mt. Sinai and talks to a monk.

THE YOUNG COUNT IS STUNNED. A PRICELESS TREASURE!

SINCE YOU'RE PLANNING TO BURN THEM, SURELY YOU WON'T MIND IF I TAKE A FEW.

NOT AT ALL. THEY HAVE NO REAL VALUE.

NINE YEARS LATER HE RETURNED FOR MORE.

I'M SORRY, MR. TISCHENDORF, WE HAVE DECIDED TO KEEP ALL OUR OLD MANUSCRIPTS.

TISCHENDORF WOULDN'T GIVE UP! FIFTEEN YEARS AFTER HIS ORIGINAL VISIT HE RETURNED AGAIN.

I HAVE AN ANCIENT GREEK TRANSLATION OF THE SCRIPTURES. WOULD YOU LIKE TO SEE IT?

I WOULD LIKE TO *STUDY* IT IF YOU DON'T MIND!

THE BOOK WAS A 4TH CENTURY GREEK COPY, THE OLDEST DISCOVERED UP TO THAT TIME!

THE OLD TESTAMENT HE FOUND WAS A VERSION CALLED THE "SEPTUAGINT," MEANING 70, BECAUSE OF THE 72 HEBREW SCHOLARS WHO ARE SAID TO HAVE TRANSLATED IT INTO GREEK.

SINCE THEN, MANY OLD TEXTS HAVE BEEN FOUND. AMONG THESE ARE THE FAMOUS DEAD SEA SCROLLS WHICH HAD BEEN HIDDEN IN CAVES ABOUT THE TIME OF CHRIST.

WHY, THIS IS THE BOOK OF ISAIAH! IT'S REMARKABLY LIKE THE TEXT IN OUR HEBREW BIBLE.

YOUNG JESUS READ THE SCRIPTURES IN HEBREW.

SCROLLS LIKE THOSE JESUS READ WERE USED AS A BASIS FOR LATER TRANSLATIONS INTO ENGLISH.

HOW WE GOT
OUR BIBLE
PART II "OUT OF MANY, ONE..."

WHEN JESUS WALKED THE EARTH, THE OLD TESTAMENT SCRIPTURES WERE WRITTEN ON LEATHER ROLLS. THE 39 BOOKS WERE DIVIDED INTO THREE PARTS: THE LAW, THE PROPHETS, AND THE WRITINGS. TOGETHER, THEY HAD ONE GREAT PURPOSE- TO MAKE GOD'S WORD KNOWN TO HIS PEOPLE. THERE WERE NO NEW TESTAMENT SCRIPTURES.

WITH THE COMING OF JESUS, PEOPLE LEARNED THAT GOD'S LOVE WAS FOR ALL MANKIND. THEY FLOCKED TO HEAR THE GOOD NEWS!

BEFORE JESUS' TIME, THE SCROLLS CONTAINING THE SCRIPTURES WERE KEPT IN SYNAGOGUES. CHOSEN READERS READ THEM ALOUD.

JESUS BROUGHT GOD'S WORD DIRECTLY TO THE PEOPLE. EVEN THE CHILDREN COULD UNDERSTAND WHAT JESUS SAID.

149

As the good news spread, the new Christians felt a need for guidance. They turned to the letters of Paul...

THE GOSPELS, THE LETTERS OF PAUL, AND OTHER WRITINGS WERE READ IN CHRISTIAN CHURCHES EVERYWHERE AND ACCEPTED AS GOD'S WORD. THEY BECAME THE NEW TESTAMENT.

THESE WORDS WERE INSPIRED BY GOD JUST AS OUR HEBREW SCRIPTURE WAS.

EARLY CHRISTIANS SUFFERED TO PRESERVE THEIR BIBLE.

SOME CHRISTIANS WERE TREATED CRUELLY BY THEIR NEIGHBORS.

ALL YOU EVER DO IS SING SONGS AND TALK ABOUT JESUS. DON'T YOU KNOW HOW TO HAVE FUN!

IT ALL DEPENDS ON WHAT YOU MEAN BY FUN!

OTHERS WERE DRIVEN FROM THEIR HOMES.

WE DON'T WANT YOUR KIND AROUND HERE!

...BOWING TO SOME FOREIGN GOD!

THEIR FAITH AND THE POWER OF THE BIBLE ITSELF KEPT THE MESSAGE ALIVE. FINALLY, THE ROMAN EMPEROR HIMSELF BECAME A CHRISTIAN.

HAVE YOU HEARD? CONSTANTINE IS A BELIEVER!

THE WHOLE EMPIRE WILL BE CHRISTIAN!

OUR PRAYERS HAVE BEEN ANSWERED!

THE DEMAND FOR BIBLES INCREASED AS THE GOOD NEWS SPREAD THROUGH THE EMPIRE.

WHY WEREN'T WE TOLD OF THIS SOONER?

NO MATTER. IT'S NEVER TOO LATE TO HEAR THE WORD OF GOD!

NEW TRANSLATIONS WERE MADE. FINALLY, A STANDARD LATIN VERSION WAS MADE.

THAT'S FATHER JEROME. HE'S BEEN WORKING FOR YEARS STUDYING SCRIPTURES IN ALL LANGUAGES.

I HEAR HE'S COME TO BETHLEHEM TO FINISH HIS WORK NEAR THE MASTER'S BIRTHPLACE.

JEROME'S LATIN BIBLE WAS USED IN EUROPE FOR A THOUSAND YEARS. IT WAS COPIED BY HAND COUNTLESS TIMES.

LITTLE BY LITTLE, PARTS OF THE BIBLE WERE TRANSLATED INTO ENGLISH. THE MORE PEOPLE HEARD THE MORE THEY WANTED!

THE FIRST COMPLETE TRANSLATION WAS MADE ABOUT 1382 BY JOHN WYCLIF.

THE PEOPLE WANT TO HEAR GOD'S WORD IN THEIR OWN LANGUAGE.

YES! WE WILL TAKE THE MESSAGE TO THE PEOPLE OURSELVES.

CHURCH OFFICIALS DIDN'T THINK THE PEOPLE SHOULD HAVE THEIR BIBLE IN ENGLISH.

WE MUST BE CAREFUL! THE BISHOP'S MEN ARRESTED FIVE OF OUR PEOPLE YESTERDAY.

AND THEY ARE DESTROYING COPIES OF OUR BIBLE.

WYCLIF SENT OUT "POOR PRIESTS" IN DEFIANCE OF THE BISHOPS TO PREACH THROUGHOUT ENGLAND!

JOHN WYCLIF DIED BUT HIS WORK WENT ON...

IT'S WRONG FOR ORDINARY PEOPLE TO READ SCRIPTURES. A LITTLE TIME IN PRISON WILL HELP YOU SEE THE ERROR OF YOUR WAYS.

MANY OF WYCLIF'S HAND-COPIED BIBLES WERE DESTROYED.

THEY CAN BURN OUR BOOKS BUT THEY CAN'T DESTROY OUR FAITH. GOD'S WORD IS FOR ALL OF US.

THE WINDS OF CHANGE WERE SWEEPING EUROPE! IN GERMANY, THE MOST EXCITING CHANGE OF ALL — THE PRINTING PRESS — DID AWAY WITH ALL NEED TO COPY THE BIBLE BY HAND.

THE VERY FIRST BOOK PRINTED ON THIS NEW MACHINE WAS THE BIBLE!

155

LATER WILLIAM TYNDALE HAD ENGLISH NEW TESTAMENTS PRINTED IN GERMANY. HE WAS FORCED TO SMUGGLE THEM INTO ENGLAND.

THE BISHOPS SENT SPIES TO TRAP TYNDALE. HE WAS FINALLY THROWN INTO PRISON.

MY WORK CONTINUES. IN THE SIXTEEN MONTHS I'VE BEEN HERE, I'VE TRANSLATED NINE OLD TESTAMENT BOOKS.

FOR HIS "HERESY" TYNDALE WAS SENTENCED TO DEATH.

LORD, OPEN THE EYES OF THE KING OF ENGLAND.

HIS PRAYER WAS QUICKLY ANSWERED!

THE BIBLE SHALL BE PRINTED IN ENGLISH AND PLACED IN EVERY CHURCH OF THE REALM. I, KING HENRY VIII, COMMAND IT!

MANY VERSIONS WERE PRINTED—THEN IN 1603, KING JAMES CAME TO THE THRONE.

WE DESPERATELY NEED A NEW TRANSLATION OF THE BIBLE.

BUT SIRE, WE HAVE TOO MANY NOW. WHAT GOOD WOULD COME OF A NEW ONE?

WE NEED ANOTHER BECAUSE THERE ARE TOO MANY. I WANT ONE BIBLE AS NEAR TO THE ANCIENT WRITINGS AS WE CAN MAKE IT!

FIFTY-FOUR SCHOLARS WORKED FOR YEARS CORRECTING OLD MISTAKES. THE RESULT WAS A NEW TRANSLATION THAT HAS BEEN USED EVER SINCE.

I WANT THE BEST SCHOLARS AVAILABLE. WE WILL DIVIDE THEM INTO SMALL GROUPS, EACH WITH A DIFFERENT PART TO WORK ON.

HOW WE GOT
OUR BIBLE
PART IV "THE BIBLE TODAY..."
THE KING JAMES BIBLE HAS BEEN USE ALL OVER THE WORLD EVER SINCE IT WAS ACCEPTED AS THE "AUTHORIZED" VERSION BY ENGLAND'S KING JAMES I IN 1611...
THE BEST GREEK AND HEBREW SCHOLARS WORKED ON IT.
THEY CHECKED EACH OTHER'S WORK. THEN OTHER SCHOLARS CHECKED AGAIN.
-AND THE KING HIMSELF, HE CALLS IT A TREASURY OF MOST COSTLY JEWELS!

THE KING JAMES VERSION WAS WRITTEN IN THE ENGLISH LANGUAGE OF 1611. SINCE THAT TIME SOME WORDS IN THE ENGLISH LANGUAGE HAVE CHANGED AND NEWER VERSIONS MAKE THE BIBLE EASIER TO READ.

THERE ARE MORE BIBLES IN ENGLISH THAN IN ANY OTHER LANGUAGE. BUT THE ENTIRE BIBLE HAS BEEN TRANSLATED INTO MORE THAN 236 DIFFERENT TONGUES.

THE PROCESS IS STILL GOING ON. NEW TRANSLATIONS ARE BEING MADE ALMOST EVERY DAY ALL OVER THE WORLD.